The Spirit Broods Over the World

The Spirit Broods Over the
WORLD

George A. Maloney, SJ

ALBA · HOUSE   NEW · YORK

SOCIETY OF ST. PAUL, 2187 VICTORY BLVD., STATEN ISLAND, NY 10314

941097

Library of Congress Cataloging-in-Publication Data

Maloney, George A., 1924 -
    The Spirit broods over the world / by George A. Maloney.
    Includes bibliographical references.
    ISBN 0-8189-0633-2
    1. Holy Spirit.   I. Title.
    BT121.2M26   1993   92-40239
    231'.3 — dc20   CIP

Imprimi Potest:
  Rev. Albert Thelen, S.J.
  Provincial of the Wisconsin Province
  of the Society of Jesus

Designed, printed and bound in the United States of
America by the Fathers and Brothers of the
Society of St. Paul, 2187 Victory Boulevard,
Staten Island, New York 10314, as part of their
communications apostolate.

PRINTING INFORMATION:

Current Printing - first digit 1 2 3 4 5 6 7 8 9 10 11 12

Year of Current Printing - first year shown
  1993   1994   1995   1996   1997   1998   1999   2000

DEDICATION

To
Sister Mary Faith, O.S.B.
of Mount Scholastica Monastery in Atchison, Kansas,
who has taught youth in the Midwest
for over fifty years in her English classes
and
in her beautiful poetry how to discover in wonderment
the brooding of the Holy Spirit.

ACKNOWLEDGMENTS

Sincere thanks to Sister Mary Faith, O.S.B. for reading and typing my manuscript; also to Dr. John Zboyovski, June Culver and Sr. Joseph Agnes of the Sisters of Charity of Halifax for their encouragement, suggestions and aid in helping me obtain certain sources needed in the writing of this book. Grateful acknowledgment is made to the publishers: Darton, Longman & Todd, Ltd., and Doubleday & Company, Inc., N.Y. for excerpts from *The Jerusalem Bible*, copyright 1966 by Darton, Longman & Todd, Ltd., and Doubleday and Company, Inc. All scriptural texts are from *The Jerusalem Bible*, unless otherwise noted.

Table of Contents

CHAPTER TWO
The Mystery Of The Trinity

CHAPTER THREE
The Holy Spirit Within The Trinity

CHAPTER FOUR
The Spirit Of God In The Old Testament

CHAPTER FIVE

The Holy Spirit In The New Testament

CHAPTER SIX

The Holy Spirit: God's Gift Of Love

CHAPTER SEVEN

The Holy Spirit Dwells Within You

CHAPTER EIGHT

The Holy Spirit Sanctifies Us

CHAPTER NINE

The Holy Spirit Fashions The Body Of Christ

Introduction

THE MYSTICAL APPROACH

AN avalanche of books and magazine articles has been published, in numbers never before seen in human history, which develop a theology of the Holy Spirit and the practical ramifications for daily living of Christians in the modern world. And here is yet another book offered to you, dear reader, on the Holy Spirit!

I hope that I have approached the subject of the Holy Spirit in a way not readily found in the popular books that have recently dealt with this topic. I have long felt that among Western Christians there has always been a penchant to objectivize the Holy Spirit through analyzing excessively the gifts, virtues and fruit of the Spirit to the loss of the *apophatic* or mysterious world of the mystical. This is surely the predominant thrust of what Scripture reveals to us about the Holy Spirit through the use of symbols. No one has ever seen God and lived (Ex 33:20). And no one can ever experience the Holy Spirit except through the working of that same Spirit.

This is also the mystical, symbolical manner used by the Eastern Christian mystical theologians who wrote and preached about the Holy Spirit. We never find in their writings a treatise analyzing the nature of the Holy Spirit as an object to be studied, or a treatise dissecting the differences among the gifts, virtues and fruit of the Spirit. It is, therefore, the scriptural and Eastern patristic writings that are the sources I have used to write this book on the Spirit.

SUMMARY OF THE BOOK

THUS I have begun this book by placing the Holy Spirit through the revelation of Jesus Christ within the source and goal of all reality, the loving community of the family of God, the Trinity. In the Spirit's kenotic or self-emptying role as the personalized love binding the Father and Son together, we see the three persons and their uniqueness in vital inter-personal relationships within the circle of love we call the Trinity.

We then turn to the Old and New Testaments to discover the revelation of the Spirit as the gentle, but powerful, presence of God as active, uncreated energies of love, touching the created world and bringing about ever increasing levels of sharing by participation through grace in God's very own family of love.

Grounded in God's revelation through Scripture, we then develop the core of the book as we study the Holy Spirit as God's personalized gift of love and immanence indwelling those who open in transcending love toward God and neighbor. Such indwelling of the Spirit within us brings about the abiding presence also of the heavenly Father and his Son, Jesus Christ.

We then study the chief work of the Spirit as Divine Love sanctifies us. We see this as the early Fathers did, as an unending process of divinization or *theosis* through the interaction of the Trinity's uncreated energies and our own cooperation with the Spirit's created sanctifying grace. This grace is always seen, not as static or mechanistic, but in the dynamics of our inter-response in self-emptying love to the indwelling Trinity as we image the Holy Spirit, a gift of love.

Finally, we climax the working of the Spirit as we ponder how the Body of Christ is being fashioned into a unity of unique individuals, living members of the Church. With particular stress in the optimism of the Pauline and Johannine writings and the commentaries of the early mystical theologians, we look into the *parousia*. This is the final, eschatological manifestation of Jesus Christ in all his members as he, in and through them in his Spirit, brings all things back to the Father in completion that will never know an end.

May these words I wrote some years ago be realized in your life, dear reader, especially through this book:

> O, beautiful Gift from God!
> I sink myself into the depths
> of that infinite love.
> I touch, dizzily, heights
> that laughingly escape my grasp.
> I plunge into depths.
> I am you!
> You are I!
>   We are God's,
> one with him!

CHAPTER ONE

The Divine Spirit Without A Face

THE INVISIBLE DIVINE PERSON

THE most invisible of the divine persons of the Trinity is the Holy Spirit. True, God is spirit and invisible and each of the three divine persons possesses a radical invisibility. Each, the Father and the Son and the Holy Spirit, can be called an invisible Spirit.

Yet the Father and the Son by their very names present to us a "face." We normally have experienced in our families a father and a child of the father. Father and Son in the Trinity are relational to each other, similar in many respects to the relationships we have experienced in our family life. We can, therefore, understand somewhat the character or personhood of the Heavenly Father and his Only Begotten Son. But the name of the Holy Spirit in no way suggests to our earthly human experiences his nature as a person in relationship to the other persons within the Trinity.

THE VISIBLE SON

THE Son of God became man and lived an earthly historical life. We can read the Gospels and imagine what kind of person Jesus historically was. That same Jesus lives now as glorified and risen from the dead. Thus we can approach the invisible God-Man with some historical, objective basis of his person-hood. John's first epistle gives us the historical Word made flesh and his relationship to us and the Father:

> Something which has existed since the beginning,
> that we have heard,
> and we have seen with our own eyes;
> that we have watched
> and touched with our hands:
> the Word, who is life —
> this is our subject.
> That life was made visible:
> we saw it and we are giving our testimony,
> telling you of the eternal life
> which was with the Father and has been made visible to us.
> What we have seen and heard
> we are telling you
> so that you too may be in union with us,
> as we are in union
> with the Father
> and with his Son Jesus Christ (1 Jn 1:1-3).

The human-divine person, Jesus Christ, comes from the Father and goes back to him (Jn 16:28). He reveals the Father with whom he was always one (Jn 1:18). He is the visible Word of the unseen Father (Col 1:15). We have no way of knowing the Father save through the Son. When the apostle Philip asked Jesus to show to him and the other disciples the Father, Jesus answered: "Who has seen me has seen the Father" (Jn 14:9).

KNOWING THE INVISIBLE FATHER

SINCE the Father has never become incarnate as did his Son, the Father, like the Holy Spirit, is invisible and without a "face." Still from our experiences of early childhood in regard to our earthly father, we have a basis of understanding the personality of the Father. Also, through his Spirit poured into our hearts, we can know by faith through the teachings of Jesus about the Father's tender, unconditional love for each of his children, what kind of personality the Father possesses.

By studying and meditating on these teachings, but, above all, by reflecting prayerfully on the earthly actions of the Word made flesh, we can understand something of the incomprehensible personhood of the eternal Father. We can believe in our Father's constant love for us as imaged by Jesus.

KNOWING THE UNKNOWN SPIRIT

BUT when we approach the subject of our knowledge of the Holy Spirit, we see that he has not been revealed as a knowable personality in a way similar to the way in which the Father and the Son have been revealed to us through the incarnate Word. Thus we cannot concretely imagine the Spirit as a real person, known to us by analogous knowledge from our own human experience.

Still the Holy Spirit is found present and actively working in the history of salvation, in both the Old and the New Testaments. The Spirit's personality is revealed to us through his activities by symbols. Although many of the scriptural images could be called "archetypal" (since all human beings have had experiences of such universal symbols as wind, breath, fire, water, tongues of fire, and a dove), these hide from us any living person. Such symbols do not refer to the inner personhood of the Holy Spirit; rather we reach a knowledge of his unique personhood by his activities or functions.

The ordinary Christian finds a grave difficulty in understanding why the third person of the Trinity should be compared to such inanimate objects as — for example — wind, breath, water, and fire. What does depicting the Holy Spirit as a dove tell us of his inner personality?[1]

Yves Congar offers other symbols that lead us into the mystery of the Holy Spirit. The Spirit in the Old and New Testaments is depicted as the "finger of God" to express his manifestation as the instrument and sign of God's power (Ex 8:15).[2] God writes the ten commandments on tablets of stone with his finger (Ex 31:19) and writes his law by the Spirit in our hearts in the New Testament.

The Spirit is called the Seal, by whom the Father anoints Christ at his Baptism (Jn 6:27); Ac 10:38) and who anoints and marks all Christians with the sign of Christ in Baptism. The Spirit is also the Gift given by the Father and Son to us. He is Peace (Jn 20:19, 21; Rm 14:17).[3]

We think also of the many other images used in the liturgy as in the hymn *Veni Creator* and the sequence *Veni, Sancte Spiritus*. The Fathers and other spiritual writers have enriched us with other symbols. For example, Symeon the New Theologian calls the Spirit the key which opens the door and St. Bernard calls the Spirit the kiss that is exchanged between the Father and the Son.[4]

NEGLECT OF THE HOLY SPIRIT

TRULY the Holy Spirit seems to us to be the most impersonal and, therefore, least relevant member of the Trinity. Arthur W. Wainright rightly observes: "The doctrine of the Holy

Spirit has long been a Cinderella of theology. It has suffered from much neglect, and has always been one of the most difficult doctrines to discuss."[5]

The doctrine of the Spirit surely has not occupied the major part of the attention of theologians. When we look at the decrees of the Second Vatican Council, we see some 158 scattered references to the Holy Spirit. Yet there is no paragraph, chapter, or decree that presents us with a unified teaching on the Holy Spirit. The non-Catholic observers, especially the Orthodox and other Oriental theologians, pointed out the seeming lack of a solid pneumatology underpinning the teachings on christology, ecclesiology, revelation, redemption, sacraments, liturgy, the ecumenical movement, and the Church in the modern world.

The doctrine of the Holy Spirit was not brought forth in any way other than as a mere addition or appendage to what the Vatican II Fathers thought to be more important topics. Pope John Paul II in his encyclical on the Holy Spirit (1986) acknowledged this grave lack of teaching on the Holy Spirit by the Council: "The christology and particularly the ecclesiology of the Council must be succeeded by a new study of and devotion to the Holy Spirit, precisely as the indispensable complement to the teaching of the Council."[6] He was quoting a statement made by Pope Paul VI in 1973 to a general audience.

We might confess that not much has been done to correct this lack of solid teaching, especially on the activities of the Holy Spirit in our individual Christian lives and in building up the Body of Christ, the Church in the modern world.[7]

Yet we see a great theological interest in the Holy Spirit arising among theologians around the world. The outburst of the charismatic renewal, especially among Catholics since 1967, but also among mainstream Protestant Churches, has brought out a rich literature dealing with the Holy Spirit in the life of the individual Christian and the gifts of the Spirit empowering Christians to witness to and live according to the guidelines of the Holy Spirit. We will discuss this in a later chapter.

WHO IS THE HOLY SPIRIT?

HOW, therefore, can we come to a right knowledge, as revealed by God, of the Holy Spirit? First, we must accept that the truth of the existence of the third person of the Trinity is at the heart of the most impenetrable divine mystery. Certitude about the existence of the Holy Spirit and his activities can never be found in the realm of speculative or positive theology. God's self-revelation in Scripture and in the apostolic teaching handed down through the magisterium of the Church makes possible a very limited positive or speculative theology.

But the highest knowledge of God, of the Trinity and of the Holy Spirit can be attained only through faith, expressed in an "apophatic" theology that opens the believer to an infused knowledge through the Spirit's gifts of the theological virtues of faith, hope, and love.

AN APOPHATIC THEOLOGY

WE have used the word "apophatic," which is a key term among the mystical writers of the Christian East, such as St. Athanasius and St. Basil, both of whom wrote the earliest treatises on the Holy Spirit. The word "apophatic" is normally used by them as the negation necessary to be added to any positive assertion about God's attributes. It is a humble confession of God's supreme transcendence that surpasses any human thought category.

We can say God is this or that, but immediately we must say, no. He is *this* but never in the way we understand. Something that we say about God and the Holy Spirit specifically may be true in some manner. Yet in another manner it is also false. God is so much more! Thus the apophatic element is more than a mere negation in the area of human linguistics. Its essential characteristic is positive.

It is a real knowing. But it is a knowing on our part through a gifted experience in love. As we stand with Moses wrapt in trembling awe before the awesome God on the mountain top, God flashes his loving presence to us through the dark cloud of unknowing. We come to know God in a new way: not merely through our rational knowledge, but in an infused knowledge that God lovingly bestows upon his children.

A PRAYERFUL, EXPERIENTIAL KNOWLEDGE

SUCH knowledge is immediate and experiential; God alone freely gives it to us when he wishes. We can never force God to give us this knowledge. God is prejudiced toward the humble, the poor in spirit, because he is truthful. He refuses to fill with himself what is already filled with selfishness.

So when we hunger and thirst for his coming, through years of obedience and cooperation with his holy will, through intense and continual purification of our hearts of all self-centeredness; in a word, when we are disposed, then God, who has always been present, reveals himself in a new way of knowing.

St. Basil in his treatise *On the Holy Spirit* describes such infused knowledge of God:

> If we are illumined by divine power, and fix our eyes on the beauty of the image of the invisible God, and through the

image are led up to the indescribable beauty of its source, it is because we have been inseparably joined to the Spirit of knowledge. He gives those who love the vision of truth the power which enables them to see the image, and this power is himself. He does not reveal it to them from outside sources, but leads them to knowledge personally. "No one knows the Father except the Son" (Mt 11:27), and "No one can say 'Jesus is Lord' except in the Holy Spirit" (1 Cor 12:3).[8]

MYSTICAL THEOLOGY

FOR the Eastern Christian mystical theologians, God, the incomprehensible One, is present and is experienced by the purified Christian. It is God's overwhelming transcendence that brings darkness to our human reasoning powers. The emphasis is not on the incapacity of human beings, but rather on the overwhelming infinity of God, always present and operating in his creation.

God's presence and transcendence are one in apophatic theology. The contemplative, the one who is given *theognosis*, knowledge about God by God directly in an experiential intuition, finds the paradox to be true, that as one comes closer to union with God, the more blinding God becomes. This is not a matter of the knowledge of God becoming more abstruse, but of the nature of God itself becoming more present by faith, hope and love. This presence is brought about by the uncreated energies of God's loving activities surrounding us at all times in every event.

Pseudo-Dionysius took the mystical doctrine of St. Gregory of Nyssa, St. Basil's brother, and incorporated it into his famous classic, *Mystical Theology*. He teaches that the way in which we approach God and are united to him is not the exclusive way of rational knowledge. It is the way of *inner vision*, though obscure to the normal, precise expectations of reason. The individual needs to be quiet and withdraw attention from sense experience and intellection.[9]

As the Christian silences his/her heart from all aggressiveness toward God and the world around self, such a person of deep prayer begins to see how bound up by shadows and darkness, by sense pleasures and false worldly values he/she really is. It is when we have the courage to confront our dark side that Jesus Christ becomes an energizing force of love as he releases his Spirit so that we can surrender to our loving Father who dwells within and calls us evermore into our true nature as being one with his only begotten Son.

THE UNAPPROACHABLE ONE

IN our brokenness we come to know that God is unreachable and unknowable by our own powers, as we are locked into the darkness of self-centered love. None of us can ever see God fully. "No one has ever seen God" (1 Jn 4:12; 1:18; 6:46; Ex 33:21). We would need to be also God, part of his essence, in order that we would know him fully. No matter how inflamed with his loving presence we may become, both in this life and in the life to come, there will always be something unfathomable about God.

GOD'S UNCREATED ENERGIES OF LOVE

THAT is why the Eastern Fathers always insisted on the distinction between God's essence and his uncreated energies. This distinction is of paramount importance. It makes possible the loving activities of the Holy Spirit, the mystical oneness of the Christian with the indwelling Trinity, and the divinization of the disciple of Christ into a child of God by participating in the very nature of God himself (2 P 1:4).

Still, our Christian faith teaches us from Scripture, God's revelation through his Word, that God in his holiness and humility wishes to share his life with us. If God is love (1 Jn 4:8), he must "go forth" out of himself to be present to another, to share his being with that other. Thus God creates the whole world in order that he may freely share himself through his gifts with human beings. Only we human beings, among all creatures, stand amidst all other creatures as the ones God has made "according to his image and likeness" (Gn 1:26).

This "going-forth" of God, to use Pseudo-Dionysius' term, is simply grace in the primal sense. It is God in his *hesed* covenantal love, pursuing his people as he stretches out his "two hands," Jesus Christ and the Holy Spirit,[10] as St. Irenaeus was fond of saying.

God, therefore, is grace as he goes out of himself in his uncreated energies to share his very own life with us. We can, then, truly know God and experience him. Although in his Godhead he is totally incomprehensible to us, yet in his energies he can be experienced. The whole message of the Good News consists in God's revelation of himself as a loving Father, giving himself to us through his son Jesus in his Spirit, and in the reality that we can truly experience such a recreating relationship of God with us. In that experience we can know God in his love toward us. We can cooperate with God's loving energies to be loving energies toward others.[11]

LOVING ENERGIES

THE energies of God flow out from the three persons within the Trinity. They are real, not material nor merely an intellectual concept. They are essential, i.e., not an accident, but they flow truly from the very essence of the Godhead. Yet they are distinct from the actual essence of the Godhead.[12] These energies are essentially personified. They are the whole Trinity acting in loving relationships toward all creatures.

In such a vision we can readily see that, for the Eastern Christian Fathers, God can never be conceived as static in his activities toward us and his created world. Because the energies are personalized, they are a common manifestation of the persons of the Trinity. If God's energies were not personalized, we would not truly share in God's very own life through his self-giving. Grace, then, would be only a mere thing God heaps upon us, different from himself the Giver. We would be justified only in an extrinsic way and not by direct contact with God's own life through his Spirit.

REVELATION THROUGH IMAGES

WE must keep in mind, therefore, that God is love and that Jesus, the only begotten Son of God incarnate, has revealed that God is also a triune community of Father, Son and Holy Spirit. Thus we see that we must balance in tension the mystery of God in self-emptying love *toward* us and the symbols that Scripture presents to us as God communicates himself to us.

The God revealed in Scripture is expressed in the symbolic language of images that must be seen, not as an objective, scientific picture of God as he really is, but of him as he is "for us" or "toward us" in his loving self-giving. St. Bernard expressed this: "I know what God is for me, but what he is for himself he knows."[13]

We mentioned already some of the images that Scripture gives us to describe the Holy Spirit, e.g., as living water or fire. Christ is called by John the Baptist the lamb of God who takes away the sins of the world (Jn 1:29). God in the Old

Testament is described as a fortress, a rock, a shepherd. These are images helpful to us to describe some active quality of the Father or Christ or the Spirit and what that relationship means to us. The Spirit is like living water insofar as he brings us into a dynamic sharing in eternal divine life.

Yet beyond such scriptural images there are Eastern Christian theologies that have developed quite differently from those developed in the Latin Roman West. When we deal with the Godhead, the Trinity, and the individual members as Father, Son and Holy Spirit, we see certain historical formulations about the divine persons that are not found literally in Scripture.

We see how St. Athanasius and the Fathers of the first ecumenical Council of Nicaea in 325 formulated a theology of the divinity of the Logos incarnate around a non-scriptural concept expressed by the Greek word *homoousios*. In the Nicene-Constantinople Creed, most Christians on Sundays recite that Jesus Christ is of the same substance or nature as is the Father: "Light from Light, true God from true God, begotten not made, of one substance with the Father. . . ." This same concept was used by the Cappadocian Fathers and the bishops gathered in the First Council of Constantinople in 381 to defend the divinity of the Holy Spirit, although literally one cannot find a statement of that divinity in the Scriptures.

Pseudo-Dionysius in the fifth century formulated the following principle: "It is important to avoid applying rashly any word or any idea at all to the super-essential and mysterious Deity apart from those divinely revealed to us in the Holy Scriptures."[14]

This is surely the reason, as Yves Congar points out,[15] why Athanasius and Basil (in their classic treatises on the Holy Spirit) and also the Fathers of the First Council of Constantinople circumvented giving the title "God" to the Holy Spirit. St. Cyril of Jerusalem was quite faithful in quoting only titles and images found in the Scripture to apply to the Spirit: "In the matter of the Holy Spirit, let us say only those things that have been written. If anything has not been written, let us not stop to investigate the fact. It is the Holy Spirit himself who dictated the Scriptures, he who has also said of himself everything that he wanted to say or everything which we are capable of grasping. Let us therefore say what he has said and let us not be so bold as to say what he has not said."[16]

NEED FOR THEOLOGY GROUNDED ON SCRIPTURE

YET we find in the history of Christian theology that theologians from both Eastern and Western traditions, the first being more mystical and liturgical and the second more analytical and rational, never in fact consistently observed literally Pseudo-Dionysius' principle. One evident reason is that our Christian faith deepens when we search. "*Fidens quaerens intellectum*"; "Faith searches for an intellectual understanding." We reach intellectually for deeper insight and connections, as we seek to plumb the depths of the mysteries hidden in Scripture.

In developing in this book a theology of the Holy Spirit and his relationships to us, we must be grounded in God's revelation in Scripture. But, also, by bringing forth the interpretations of the magisterium, especially as found in the great ecumenical councils and in the writings of the leading theologians and mystics of both East and West, we can discover exciting and relevant truths about the Holy Spirit in vital relationships to us.

Hilary of Poitiers in his work on the Trinity points out how theologians had to come to the defence of certain basic truths, for example the divinity of Jesus Christ and of the Holy Spirit, and had to place boundaries or "definitions" in the strict sense of the word to ward off any heresies that rose up to attack the essentials of Christianity. He writes:

> The guilt of heretics and blasphemers compels us to undertake what is unlawful, to scale arduous heights, to speak of the ineffable, and to trespass upon forbidden places. And since by faith alone we should fulfill what is commanded, namely, to adore the Father, to venerate the Son with him, and to abound in the Holy Spirit, we are forced to raise our lowly words to subjects which cannot be described. By the guilt of another we are forced into guilt, so that what should have been restricted to the pious contemplation of our minds is now exposed to the dangers of human speech.[17]

A WAITING IN INNER POVERTY

IT was necessary, therefore, to present in this chapter the symbols and images that in Scripture reveal to us something about the Holy Spirit, not in his essence, but in his dynamic activities toward us and the created world. This is a preamble to a theology of the Holy Spirit that will aid us to live in a loving response to God's Spirit as his gift of love to us through his Son.

Now we are ready to begin our probe into the Holy Spirit, the member of the Trinity who has no "face," and who admits of no "personalized" relationships to the Father and the Son other than that of proceeding or issuing forth in love from them to us human beings. Let us keep always in mind an *apophatic theology* that respects what the Holy Spirit has revealed in the symbols of Scripture and that is open to a sense of mystery. Thus we can begin our theological search to know the Holy Spirit as he manifests himself in power and tender love to us in our history of salvation.

That beginning hurls us through infinite spaces and all times back to the eternity before God ever fashioned and still fashions this universe as he "goes forth" to "other" himself and his infinite beauty in the participated beauties of his created world.

It is there within the Trinity of an I-Thou-We community that we must first contemplate the activities of the Holy Spirit as the Gift of bonding love between the Father and the Son. For the very Gift of God's Spirit to us is the Gift that "goes forth" in self-emptying love from the father to the Son. The true nature of love is not to have a "face," but to be experienced in the *kenotic* or self-emptying between two persons. No image, no word, no symbol or sign can truly surround the Holy Spirit with seeming mental walls that shout out: "Here we have captured God's Spirit! He is here and not there. He is this and not that." In humility we approach the Burning Bush, take off our shoes and fall down in adoration to be enlightened by the invisible Spirit of God, who is always operating as loving activity in every facet of God's created world. His works of love are visible and experienced only in our intimate oneness with him as we purify ourselves of our own deluded power to know him as an object. In utter emptiness of heart we wait for the wind, the fire, the living waters to rush upon us and reveal himself in deed.

CHAPTER TWO

The Mystery Of The Trinity

EXPERIENCING THE TRINITY

ONLY if God ravishes us shall we be what he created us to be. In the words of St. Irenaeus, we are empty receptacles to be filled by God. God first freely creates us; then freely he seeks to communicate himself to us as intellectual beings, capable of hearing his Word and in his Spirit of love to be transformed into regenerated children of God and to return his love. All this is in order that God may share his very trinitarian life with us.

Let us look at the mystery of the Trinity in order to lay the groundwork for God's communication unto intimate communion in his Word through his Holy Spirit. For it is the very same Father, Son and Holy Spirit of the Trinity who come and dwell within us and share their divine life with us. This is the incredibly Good News that the God-Man, Jesus Christ, makes possible through his revelation by his Spirit.

There burns within our hearts a desire to "experience" God. Like Moses, we too have tried to approach the "Burning

Bush" by our own power. We have sought to touch and handle the Absolute by means of our own images and ideas. Yet God, "a consuming fire" (Heb 12:29), defies such cardboard constructions in his beyondness and unpossessableness.

A REVEALED MYSTERY

THE mystery of the Trinity has been revealed to us in Holy Scripture. Revelation is a communication, a manifestation of truths by God who makes them known to us. God positively intervenes to disclose to human beings truths by means of signs. And so we can know much about God through his revelation in his created, material world. He reveals more of himself to his chosen people through the Law and the Prophets.

But it is when his Word becomes incarnate that the Father most fully reveals himself, no longer in words and signs, but in the one Word and Sacrament, Jesus Christ. We have no way of knowing the Father, but through seeing him in his Son (Jn 14:9). We have no way of receiving God's love for us except through receiving the personalized love of Jesus Christ. "As the Father loves me, so I love you" (Jn 15:9). The Son reveals the Father to us through the Holy Spirit.

If God is love by essence, then he is always seeking by his nature to share his being by communicating his presence. The Father communicates himself through his Word in his Spirit of love. God creates the whole world as good, as a sign of his burning desire to give himself in faithful communication through the Word. The world at its interior is filled with the self-communicating Trinity. God's uncreated energies swirl through and fill all creatures with his loving, creative presence (Ps 33:4-9). The Father delights to give himself through his Word to his creatures.

> . . . I was by his side, a master craftsman,
> delighting him day after day,
> ever at play everywhere in his world,
> delighting to be with the sons of men (Pr 8:29-31).

Everything flows out of the Father's exuberant fullness of being and becomes a reality in his communicating Word. He speaks through his Word and oceans and mountains, birds and beasts, flowers and all living things spring into being under his laughing, joyful gaze. Nothing that is can escape his loving touch, his presence as Giver of life. Not only does God communicate himself in creation, but he is a sustaining, directing God.

The Father's fullest revelation is made in his incarnate Word, Jesus Christ. For in him we have not only words, but we have the one Word that is the perfect copy of the Father's nature. In him we can come not only to know God's very nature, but we can be brought into a loving communion with God's being. We can become truly participators of God's very own nature (2 P 1:4). The Letter to the Hebrews describes this revelation in God's incarnate Word (Heb 1:1-4).

Knowing the Word incarnate, we can now know the Father and his Spirit in whom the Word makes known to us the Father. By listening to the Word enfleshed for love of us, we can know what the inner life of the Trinity is like. It is through the Word made flesh that we can learn of the communitarian sharing within the Trinity which is the model of the same trinitarian energies of love that are shared with us human beings *ad extra*, outside of that "essential" life of the Triune God. We can be caught up in the absolute reality that is at the heart of all other reality, that which is the beginning and the end of all being.

God the Father, the "unoriginated Source of being," in absolute silence, in a communication of love impossible for human beings to understand, speaks his one eternal Word through his Spirit of love. In that one Word, the Father is perfectly present, totally self-giving to his Son. "In him lives the fullness of divinity" (Col 2:9).

In his Spirit, the Father also hears his Word come back to him in a perfect, eternal "yes" of total surrendering love that is again the Holy Spirit. The Trinity is a reciprocal community of a movement of the Spirit of Love between Father and Son. Our weak minds cannot fathom the peace and joy, the ardent excitement and exuberant self-surrender that flow in a reposeful motion between Father and Son through the Holy Spirit.

Such an entrance on our part into the very nature of God and his trinitarian community of three relational persons is impossible outside of God's revelation. The doctrine of the Trinity and God's one nature is a truth impossible to be grasped by our natural composition. M.J. Scheeben writes:

> Without belief in God's revelation it cannot be known at all; and even for believers it is incomprehensible in an exceptionally high degree, indeed, in the highest degree. There it is a mystery in the truest, highest, most beautiful sense of the word. [1]

THE GODHEAD AS SOURCE

BEFORE God moves out in loving relationships, even within the Trinity, it is impossible to conceive of what the early Eastern Fathers knew as the Godhead. This is, in the words of the 14th century Rhenish mystic, Meister Eckhart, the "unnatured nature" of God. Mystics referred to this absolutely unknowable God, prior to a loving movement of person to person, as the Abyss, the Desert, the Wilderness, the Absolute beyond any being. This is motionless unity and balanced stillness.[2] It is the fullness of being that has not yet spilled out as loving Gift.

This is infinite Zero, for out of this infinite potentiality all other beings emanate and have their being. The concept is in no way negative. Rather, it symbolizes the fullness which embraces all being and hence cannot even be given the name of being.

The Godhead is the "unmanifested" or "undifferentiated" dimension of God's nature, in the words of Pseudo-Dionysius.[3] No name can truly be given to the Godhead for it is a nameless form, the Ultimate Ground, out of which all other beings come. It is the Absolute Beginning, the Immovable Rest from which all movement and differentiation in being come.

In the Godhead is the fullness of being, the Silence out of which will come relational communication. God as Stillness is the Godhead waiting to move from Silence to Speech, from perfect repose and motionlessness to sharing love in movement towards Another.

THE REVEALING SON AND SPIRIT

THE Godhead that moves toward expression and intelligibility or meaningfulness does so in the relationship of the Godhead as Father knowing himself in his full meaning, and his Son through his Spirit of love. This is not only a meaningfulness toward us creatures in the order of salvation, but it is the Son in his eternal "imaging" of the Father's love through the Holy Spirit, who gives to the Godhead as Father his full meaning. The Father knows himself only in his image, his Son through his Spirit. The Godhead concentrates his entire essence in the Son that allows the Father to become the knower and the Son as known, but also vice versa: the Son in the Spirit is the knower as he knows the Father to be his total Source and Origin of being and the Father is known as Father.

But this inter-relationship between the Father and Son in self-knowledge cannot be possible except through the Holy Spirit. This is why there must be a triple movement within the one Godhead. It is the Holy Spirit who eternally illumines the mystery for the Father and the Son. St. Hilary of Poitiers insists that the Father and the Son have a perfect, mutual knowledge, which exists because of their mutual relationship of Father and Son to each other.[4] If the Father and Son mutually know themselves, this knowledge is brought about necessarily by the Holy Spirit. The Father and Son, knowing themselves in that primal act of "emptying" of the Father into the Son and the Son into the Father in mutual self-surrender is nothing but the binding force of the Holy Spirit as Love. The Holy Spirit cannot be an accidental relation, a "thing" produced, even from all eternity. In a mysterious manner the Holy Spirit unites the Father and Son eternally in love that cannot be separated from the knowing by the Father in his Son. The Spirit makes it possible that the unity of the Godhead can be still shared without destroying that unity in the diversity of persons who share in that essence.

THE I IS THE CHILD OF WE

GABRIEL Marcel's famous statement: "The I is the child of the We"[5] has its fullest meaning within the trinitarian relationships. God as Trinity is the revelation that uniqueness of persons comes only from a family of two or more persons in love. In the very self-giving of the Father to the Son and the Son to the Father, a third person has his being. The Holy Spirit proceeds as the Love between the Father and the Son.

From this three-fold movement, therefore, all reality flows within the Trinity and without, i.e., in the order of creation and God's shared being through his uncreated energies of love. The Divine Logos is the natural and perfect expression of the Father and is naturally and perfectly expressed by the Love of the Father that is the Spirit. Knowledge is not enough, but it must be completed by love since it exists in that first movement of self-giving. Love completes the knowledge and although knowledge and love are not the same, within the Trinity both the Son as known in the love of the Father and as knowing the Father in his returned love can be possible only through realized love which is the Spirit proceeding from the Father along with the Son. Yet both proceed differently from the one Source.

AN UNCHANGING MOVEMENT

THIS eternal movement within the Trinity is totally an immanent action that knows no finite beginning, increase, or cessation. It is an eternal "insession" or, to use the word coined by the early Greek Fathers, a "perichoresis." It is a relational inter-penetration of all three Persons, distinct by their oppositional relationships. Yet all are one in the very knowing and loving that each possesses in the same nature.

This "perichoresis" in knowledge and love, in unity and distinction, is the basis for God's trinitarian "inter-penetration" within us as human beings as the trinitarian indwelling, as will be developed later. God's humility in sharing his being with us human beings is to be found in his humble, "homely" love, to quote Julian of Norwich's striking phrase. This "homely" love is God calling us into his very own family, God's home. To make his home with us is to take us into his very own "family." He allows us to participate in his very own nature as 2 P 1:4 says.

Within the Trinity, therefore, because of God's humility in wanting to know and love himself in his Son and Spirit, we find the basis of all reality. Love becomes energized love when it is an actualized sharing of one's being with another. True love always is rooted in humble self-giving. And thus, at the heart of all reality in the Christian view is the eternal Father wanting to have no being except in his begetting into being his eternal Son. Panikkar has caught this thought in what he terms "the Cross in the Trinity":

> In the Father the apophatism (the *kenosis* or emptying of Being) is real and total. This is what elsewhere I have called "the Cross in the Trinity" i.e., the integral immolation of God, of which the Cross of Christ and his immolation are only the images and revelations. [6]

Jesus Christ, the Word of God incarnate and perfect image of the Heavenly Father in human form, became that perfect expression of the Father's love, both for himself and for all of us loved by the Father in his Word (Ph 2:6-11). We can thus understand why his awesome kenosis on the Cross tells us something of the Father's self-giving within the Trinity, the basis of all true self-giving and of the grace that make all human loves and self-giving possible.

Let us now turn to the role of the Holy Spirit within the Trinity as the basis for our knowledge of him in his activities in relationship to us human beings.

CHAPTER THREE

The Holy Spirit Within The Trinity

THE MYSTERY REVEALED

FROM the two preceding chapters we can see that the ineffable mystery of the Trinity, which escapes our own human comprehension, can, however, be known and experienced in and through Jesus Christ and the Holy Spirit. God not only deigned to reveal the truth of this mystery to us but in that revelation he has made the mystery of the Trinity the beginning and the end of all reality. God effects our fulfillment precisely in and through the activities of the triune God in the context of our history of salvation.

THE ECONOMY OF SALVATION

WE come, not only to know, but also to experience the triune God within what Karl Rahner calls the biblical data about the "economic" Trinity. "Economia" (*oikonomia* in Greek) refers to any divine activity in relationship to creatures. Thus theologian speaks of "the economy of salvation." Among the early Eastern Fathers, theology properly so-called concerns itself with teaching about the Divine Being itself, namely, the immanent Holy Trinity. The exterior manifestations of God, the Holy Trinity known in its relation to created being, belong to the realm of economy.[1]

It is in the context of the relationships of the Trinity toward the created world, especially to human beings, that Karl Rahner states very emphatically his principle: "The 'economic Trinity' is the 'immanent Trinity' and the 'immanent Trinity' is the 'economic Trinity.' "[2] Such a thesis is solidly rooted also in the Eastern patristic theologizing about the mystery of the Trinity in relationship to us. There must be a connection between the Trinity and ourselves. In identifying the economic Trinity with the immanent Trinity, Rahner, along with the Eastern Fathers as well as M. Scheeben, seeks to stress the personalism of the three divine persons in their one "essential" act of self-communication to human beings. If this were not so, Rahner argues, "God would be the 'giver,' not the *gift itself*; he would 'give himself' only to the extent that he communicates a gift distinct from himself."[3]

A very important question hinges upon this thesis of the similarity between the immanent, trinitarian "activities" and the economic "activities." Are we so loved by God that we are radically transformed by God's gift of himself and by his very own transforming Persons, the Son and the Holy Spirit? Or are we merely extrinsically "affiliated" with God in a salvation of decree and not of true "regeneration"?

The early Fathers lived daily in the mystery of the triune God through experiencing God as energies of love. They knew that they could never know or experience the essence of God which always remained unknowable and incomprehensible to created man. This is what Karl Rahner calls the "immanent" Trinity. But they knew from Holy Scripture, especially through the work of Jesus Christ and his Holy Spirit, that God does communicate himself to us in a new knowing and a new participation through his energies. These energies are God's mode of existing in relationship to his created world, especially to human beings. These energies are not *things*, as an extrinsic "grace" that God heaps upon us, but they are truly God himself as *Gift*.

Roland Zimany accurately describes the distinction between God's essence and his energies:

> God, the essential Trinity, is the Giver, and God in his energies, which enable God to be known outside himself and which are inseparable from the divine nature which they manifest, is the gift of uncreated grace.[4]

DIVINIZATION

WITH the divine energies always surrounding us and lovingly calling us to respond to God's Word living within us and within the context of our existential life, we reach our highest development in the continued cooperation (*synergy*) with God's energetic presence. When we continuously cooperate with God's grace (his divine, uncreated energies manifested to us in the context of our daily lives), we enter into the process of *theosis* or divinization which is the total integration of the body-soul-spirit relationships of us with God. This is the end of God's creation of us human beings as his masterpiece, endowed with an orientation to grow daily into the image and likeness of God that is Jesus Christ.

This trinitarian movement indwells and sweeps us up into an unchanging, yet always freshly new action of divine

self-giving in the deepest communion possible to us human
beings. But first, we must seek to understand what revelation
has given us about the immanent life of the Holy Spirit in his
relationships with the Father and Son, since the Spirit operates
toward us in the "economic" order as he is constituted a unique
person in relationship to the Father and the Son within the
"immanent" order within the Trinity. The Spirit reveals to us,
not the Father, but the mutual love of the Father and Son for us.
Only the Son could have communicated what the Heavenly
Father feels in love toward us, since the Son is the Word that
communicates the divine Mind of the Father to us. But the
Spirit reveals to us the Father and the Son's mutual love
perfectly only when Jesus Christ had died on the cross. As
Scheeben puts it:

> In the Godhead the mutual love of the Son and the Father
> pours itself out in the production of the Holy Spirit, who
> issues from their common heart, in whom both surrender their
> heart's blood, and to whom they give themselves as the pledge
> of their infinite love. In order worthily to represent this
> infinitely perfect surrender to His Father, the Logos wished in
> His humanity to pour forth His blood from His heart to the last
> drop, that blood in which and through which the Holy Spirit
> gave life to His humanity, the blood that was pervaded,
> sanctified, and scented with heavenly loveliness, and so
> ascended to God with such pleasing fragrance. . . . He [the
> Spirit] urges on the God-man to His sacrifice, and brings the
> oblation itself into the presence of the Father, uniting it to the
> eternal homage of love, which is He Himself. [5]

INTER-PERSONAL RELATIONS

ONE of the key models used in Trinitarian theology, both in
the East and in the West, is that proposed and developed in

detail by St. Augustine and repeated by St. Thomas Aquinas. It has been called the "psychological image" of the Trinity found within the very reflective process of the human person concerning his or her own consciousness. St. Augustine describes this analogy: "For we both are, and know that we are, and delight in our being, and know our knowledge of it."[6] The Father is the Source of being, the Son is associated with the Father's knowing of himself in his Word, and the Spirit is the Love of the Father knowing himself in his Word. Karl Rahner and a host of modern theologians find this model quite inadequate to express the dynamic inter-personal relations that exist among Father, Son and Holy Spirit.[7] H. Mühlen finds this model's inadequacy to consist in its weakness to explain the spiration of the Holy Spirit.[8]

Perhaps a model proposed by Richard of St. Victor (+1173) can serve to avoid the scholastic language of viewing the inner Trinitarian relations in a static manner and put us in touch with a more biblical and Greek patristic approach. We can relate more deeply to this model as it is built upon the mystery of love relationships. Richard bases his understanding of the Trinity on the premise that true love seeks to be totally self-sacrificing on behalf of the one loved. But such a love wants to be shared with another, thus an *I* and *Thou* move into a *We*-community of three persons equally loving each other with the very same love. He writes:

> When one gives love to another and when he alone loves the other alone, there is love certainly but not shared love. When two love each other and give each other their most ardent affection and when the affection of the first flows to the second and that of the second to the first, moving as it were in different directions, there is love on both sides certainly, but there is not shared love. Strictly speaking, there is shared love when two persons love a third in a harmony of affection

and a community of love they have for the third. . . . From
this, then, it is evident that shared love would not have a place
in the divinity if there were only two persons and not a third.[9]

THE SPIRIT OF GOD

BUT if there were only the Father and the Son, there would be
no community of two persons giving themselves to each other
and fructifying in a third. There would be no movement outside
of a mutual desire toward *union.* The result would not only be a
denial of the Trinity but a negation of a God who has so loved as
to give us his only begotten Son so that in his Gift, the Spirit of
love, we might have eternal life (Jn 3:16).

Richard of St. Victor shows that God must enjoy the
highest degree of love, *agape*, since God is perfect goodness.
But true love in its perfect manifestation is a love that moves
away from self to communicate itself to another. Any love that
does not go beyond itself is still imperfect.[10] But in God such
another person to whom God gives himself cannot be a created
person, since God would be loving that person infinitely and
perfectly but in an inordinate way. The loveableness of the
second person would have to be in proportion to God's love.
The second person of the Trinity, for Richard, is that "co-
worthy" person and, therefore, he himself is also God. Thus it
seems as though perfect love would demand at least two divine
persons of equal worth.

But true love is driven to a transcendence that wants love
received to be shared by a third person. Richard argues for the
existence within the Trinity of the Holy Spirit on the basis of
the psychology of love. The Son wants to love the Father with a
perfect, mutual love, just as the Father loves him.[11] It would
be an imperfection between the Father and the Son if they did
not want to share their love with another. But to share this

mutual love there is need of a *condilectum*, one that is loved equally as the Father loves the Son and the Son loves the Father. This is the Holy Spirit.[12]

THE I-THOU-WE IN MARRIAGE

THE parallel with human love found in marriage is a powerful argument from experience for the Trinity. As the Father and Son wish to perfect their love by sharing it with the Holy Spirit, so do a husband and wife wish to fashion a community of at least three by a child. Two in love move toward union, but only in the sharing of their mutual love with a third person does their union become fulfilled. This parallel is found also in God's salvific designs on the human race, beginning with his chosen people. His perfect love outside the Trinity is a reflection of that community of love, not only desiring union with his people, but actually effecting a union in the fashioning of a third entity that can share their love. God's love for the human race would be incomplete if he would not by grace wish to share his very own love and life by making us his children through the incarnate Son and Holy Spirit.

Today there is a great stress being placed on inter-personal relations. Father Heribert Mühlen has brought about an exciting synthesis of the insights of past theologians, such as St. Augustine, Richard of St. Victor, St. Thomas Aquinas and Duns Scotus, to highlight the inter-personal relationships within the Trinity.[13] Mühlen takes many insights from the metaphysics of language as developed by Dietrich von Hildebrand[14] and Wilhelm von Humboldt[15] in order to show the distinctive personality of the Holy Spirit as coming out of an *I-Thou* relationship between Father and Son.

Before we move into such a description of the Holy Spirit in terms of inter-personal relationships, let us see some of the past difficulties that concern the Holy Spirit, especially those coming from Holy Scripture. Surely for most of us there is little difficulty in understanding the Son-relationship, both from Holy Scripture and dogmatically within the Trinity itself. This Son has become incarnate and has spoken about himself. In regard to the Father, the Son has revealed to us what he is like. Added to this revelation, we have a "natural" revelation of such an *I-Thou* relationship in our natural existence of being sons and daughters of an earthly father and mother.

But when we seek to probe deeper into the meaning of the Holy Spirit, both within the Trinity and within our own spiritual life, we find many difficulties. Historically in the great ecumenical councils the dogma about the divinity of the Holy Spirit and his relationship with the Father and Son was articulated after the great christological dogmas had been clarified. This no doubt is due to the lack of clarity found in Holy Scripture. But it also means that a doctrine which depends totally upon other doctrines cannot be clarified until such prior doctrines have been clearly enunciated. The implications of the Holy Spirit could have been drawn only when the full divinity of the Son, of the same nature as the Father, an equal *I-Thou* community, was firmly established.

AN I-THOU-WE-COMMUNITY

THE greatest deterrent in presenting the Holy Spirit as the transforming love of the Father and the Son that divinizes us into the very community of the Trinity came, however, through the scholastic presentation both of the Holy Spirit and of the Trinity. The four Aristotelian categories to explain any causality (material, formal, efficient and final causes) were used to explain the actions of the Trinity outside of itself toward the created world, but also to describe the operations of the individual divine persons indwelling us through created grace. Created grace, as habitual and sanctifying, was objectivized away from the personal love relationships of the trinitarian persons toward us.

Mühlen helps us to recapture the insights of Holy Scripture and allows us also to interpret grace primarily — as the Greek Fathers did — as the uncreated energies of the total God-community meeting us individuals with the undividuated, personalized relationships of each trinitarian person. According to the insight of von Humboldt,[16] that speech can arise only through the mediation of a duality. Mühlen shows how the Father and the Son say an *I* and a *Thou* relationship. We have pointed out how the Father knows himself in his Word and Son, and the Son knows himself only in the Father. The Holy Spirit brings about a *We* relationship.

Dietrich von Hildebrand explains how the *We*-relationship builds upon the *I-Thou* as the foundation, making the *We*-relationship a community of an *I-Thou* with a third in a "common performance of acts and attitudes."[17]

The Father not only knows himself in his Son, but he also acknowledges himself as uniquely the Son's Father. The opposition between the Father and Son only increases the intimacy the more each person acknowledges both his own uniqueness and that of the other. As the uniqueness of each person increases the intimacy and the desire for greater union, love is generated and brings about the union. But this love cannot be a thing in the Trinity. It must be the personalized Act of Love coming out of the mutual love of the Father and Son, loving each other in "our Spirit." The Spirit "proceeds" from the union of the two uniquely different persons, Father and Son. The Spirit's being as a person within the Trinity consists in being the act of union and distinction between the Father

and Son, and in this "action" the Spirit finds his "personality."
Thus the Spirit can never be considered apart from either the
Father or the Son.

FILIOQUE

SPEAKING the Word in eternal silence through his outpouring Love that is his Holy Spirit, the Heavenly Father hears his
Word come back to him in a perfect, eternal, "yes" of total,
surrendering Love, that is again the Holy Spirit. The theological controversy between the Orthodox and Catholic Churches
about the *Filioque* (whether the Holy Spirit proceeds from the
Father alone or also from the Son) is no controversy when
contemplated in the eternal begetting of God's Word in God's
Love. Both Churches hold a partial statement of the truth. The
contemplative, who stands before this sacred mystery, knows
in a knowledge given only by God's Spirit that the Holy Spirit
proceeds as Love from the Father, and in that same proceeding
act of Love the Word is eternally spoken, known and loved.
But the Son echoes this Divine Love as He, the Word, goes
back to the Father in the same Divine Spirit. The Spirit
originates from the Father, but through the mediation of the
Son that forms the *I-Thou* community and through the Spirit
attains a *We*-community. The Spirit also proceeds back to the
Father as the Word's loving response. The Holy Spirit is the
silent gasp of mutual, loving surrender between Father and
Son in a community of *We*. He brings to completion the divine
union between Father and Son in the ecstasy of shared love.
    It is this moving of God's *We*-community toward mankind
in order to give us a share in the life of the three persons
through the Spirit of the risen Jesus that is at the heart of the
Christian message. St. Paul sums it up in non-speculative,
scriptural terms:

Blessed be God the Father of our Lord Jesus Christ, who has blessed us with all the spiritual blessings of heaven in Christ. Before the world was made, he chose us, chose us in Christ, to be holy and spotless, and to live through love in his presence, determining that we should become his adopted sons, through Jesus Christ . . . to make us praise the glory of his grace, his free gift to us in the Beloved. . . . He has let us know the mystery of his purpose, the hidden plan he so kindly made in Christ from the beginning . . . that he would bring everything together under Christ, as head, everything in the heavens and everything on earth. . . . Now you too, in him, have heard the message of the truth and the good news of your salvation, and have believed it; and you too have been stamped with the seal of the Holy Spirit of the Promise, the pledge of our inheritance which brings freedom for those whom God has taken for his own, to make his glory praised (Eph 1:3-14).

CHAPTER FOUR

The Spirit Of God In The Old Testament

LOVE IS AT THE CENTER

YOU and I have been made for the greatest reality in the world and that is love. The main driving force in our lives is to experience such love and to express it to those who enter into our lives. We obtain meaningfulness and ultimate worth only in the degree of love received and accepted by us from others and through our gifts of love to others.

The love at the center of the universe, that lives and moves within us and around us in self-giving, is, first and last, the triune God. This self-giving, self-sharing, is a community of an *I-Thou* in a *We* family. It is the hidden presence of God's love between Father and Son that is personalized and called the Holy Spirit. This Spirit is the presence of God's love, found at the core of the entire world's reality and in our hearts.

This voice of love speaks in the Scriptures of the Old and

New Testaments, but also wherever men and women live in unselfish love for others. God's loving voice is speaking in our modern age as we are taught by this Spirit to live in God's truth and love.

GOD'S RUAH-BREATH IN ALL OF CREATION

GOD'S burning love sears through every part of our being. His Spirit of love is not far from any of us. In this ocean of love we live and move and have our being (Ac 17:28). Yet God reveals his loving presence to us in a progressive way that starts in Scripture in the Old Testament with basic signs and symbols that stress God's loving action in every detail of our lives.

God's Spirit is depicted in the Old Testament by the primal symbol of wind or breath. This in Hebrew is the oft repeated word *ruah* (in Greek, *pneuma*), found 178 times in the Old Testament.[1] In a progressive revelation of the all-pervasive, active presence of God's love, the Holy Spirit, the more ancient texts first describe God's Spirit as wind or breath or air. Nomadic peoples as the Israelites, living in the desert, know from daily experience the life-giving power of desert winds which bring rain-filled clouds and life-giving waters.

God's loving activities in Israel's history are typified as a mighty wind or breath coming out of God's very own being (Ex 15:10) that filled the Jews with a humble reverence. The wind, therefore, is the breath of God working powerfully in his created world, especially in the hearts of human beings, made in his image and likeness (Gn 1:26).

God was meant to be our very own breath. We were to be healthy and full of life by breathing in the loving power of God. Breath is one of the most primal symbols of life as given to us by God. When we no longer breathe, we are dead.

We can say that our breath is in a way a part of God. "By

the word of Yahweh the heavens were made, their whole array by the breath of his mouth" (Ps 33:6). The Jews of the Old Testament never consider God in a static way, as merely being "up there" or "over there," like an object, but as a personalized energy of love, interacting with all his creatures. He leads the universal dance of all things in harmonious yet individualized motion, stretching toward greater complexity and yet greater union in multiplicity.

GOD IS THE VERY BREATH WE BREATHE

THE Jews understood that at all times God was giving them life, as seen by the breath they breathed. Job calls us back to our complete dependence upon God: "He holds in his power the soul of every living thing, and the breath of each man's body" (Jb 12:10). "I was fashioned out of clay. God's breath it was that made me, the breathing of Shaddai that gave me life" (Jb 33:4).

The Greeks thought more philosophically in dealing with man and God and the "essence" of each creature. The Jews were not as analytical but more experiential in approaching God as the Source of all life and creation. God for them was a vital force, energy and principle of all action, even as the one at the center of evil, not as its creator, but as the primary source of all that is and out of which he can draw good, even from evil. The spirit-breath of God, as Yves Congar describes the understanding of the Jews, is what animates and causes to act in order to realize God's plan. It is always a life-energy.[2]

Job confesses that "as long as a shred of life is left in me, and the breath of God breathes in my nostrils . . ." he would live (Jb 27:3). God exhales and his breath puts life into all his creatures. When God inhales and withdraws his breath, they die:

> You turn your face away, they suffer.
> You stop their breath, they die
> and revert to dust.
> You give breath, fresh life begins,
> you keep renewing the world (Ps 104:29-30).

Jean Danielou contrasts what he considers the more holistic spirituality of the Jews with the approach of the Greeks to spirituality:

> What do we mean when we speak of "spirit" and say that "God is spirit"? Are we speaking Greek or Hebrew? If we are speaking Hebrew, we are saying that God is a storm and an irresistible force. This is why, when we speak of spirituality, a great deal is ambiguous. Does spirituality mean becoming immaterial or does it mean being animated by the Holy Spirit?[3]

Thus we see the rather "earthly" way of the Jews in describing God's Spirit as the source of all life. Life can never be something we human beings can possess independently of God. "It is Yahweh who speaks, who spread out the heaven and founded the earth and formed the spirit of man within him" (Zc 12:1).

A CREATIVE PRESENCE OF GOD IN ALL THINGS.

GOD'S Spirit is always seen by the Old Testament Jews as the exterior power and source of all life, different from man's spirit. Before God creates man and woman and calls them to be co-creators by "en-spiriting" them with an intimate sharing through the gifts of intellect and will, God is seen hovering over the chaos in the beginning of creation (Gn 1:2), ready to stir the cosmos out of its slumbering impotence to fullness of life. "Now the earth was a formless void, there was darkness over the deep, and God's spirit hovered over the water" (Gn 1:2).

We must be aware that *ruah-breath/spirit* in the Old Testament is never seen as opposing the material, the corporeal or the body. Thus we see the beautiful image of God's creative power transcendentally hovering over the chaos. God loves his creation. He breathes his own life into all facets of creation. The *ruah-breath* of the Old Testament is never disincarnate.[4]

Psalm 147 captures well God's Spirit operating immanently inside of his creation in all ordinary events of reality:

> He gives an order;
> his word flashes to earth:
> to spread snow like a blanket,
> to strew hoarfrost like ashes,
> to drop ice like breadcrumbs,
> and when the cold is unbearable,
> he sends his word to bring the thaw
> and warm wind to melt the snow (Ps 147:15-17).

No wonder Jesus could preach: "Why, every hair on your head has been counted. . . . Now if that is how God clothes the grass in the field which is there today and thrown into the furnace tomorrow, how much more will he look after you, you men of little faith!" (Lk 12:7, 28).

GOD'S SPIRIT AND THE HUMAN SPIRIT

THE "second creation" account in Genesis[5] shows us a most intimate relationship of God's Spirit to human beings, different from his relationship with the rest of sub-human creation:

> Yahweh God fashioned man of dust from the soil. Then he
> breathed into his nostrils a breath of life, and thus man
> became a living being (Gn 2:7).

This passage from Genesis describes a twofold relationship. Man is shown to be made out of earth-matter and, therefore, has his roots with the rest of material creation. But Yahweh breathes into man his very own spark of divinity. When man acts according to the "flesh," he places himself as the center and source of his own life. He destroys the responsibility God entrusted to him to be a creative steward by living and working creatively according to God's spark within him.

By God's life which he breathes over the sub-human creation, all other material creatures are complete in their relationship of dependence upon God. An oak tree cannot will to be a pine tree. Yet when God breathes into "the nostrils" of man a breath of life, God exercises a new creative act that sets the human person completely off from the rest of creation.

Michelangelo, in his famous Sistine Chapel painting of God's creation of man, pictures God as descending and touching man. God creates man as an "unfinished" being, one who in his first moments of existence immediately has a relation of person to person with God.

Emil Brunner beautifully describes this ontological relationship to God through God's Word in his Spirit:

> God creates man in such a way that in this very creation man
> is summoned to receive the Word actively, that is, he is called
> to listen, to understand, and to believe. God creates man's
> being in such a way that man knows that he is determined and
> conditioned by God and in this fact is truly human. The being
> of man as an "I" is being from and in the Divine "Thou," or,
> more exactly, from in the Divine Word, whose claim 'calls'
> man's being into existence. . . . The characteristic imprint of

man, however, only develops on the basis of Divine determination, as an answer to a call, by means of a decision. The necessity for decision, an obligation which he can never evade, is the distinguishing feature of man . . . it is the being created by God to stand 'over-against him,' who can reply to God, and who in this answer alone fulfills — or destroys — the purpose of God's creation.[6]

God is the very ground of man's being. Man has been created by God's ever constant, never changing, present-now act of love. And we human beings never live outside of the glow of this Spirit of love. The Spirit is constantly ordering us toward a personal response of "yes" to the invitation that we become like to the Father's image and likeness that is his divine Son. St. Paul phrases it thus: "And you have put on a new self which will progress toward true knowledge the more it is renewed in the image of its creator" (Col 3:10).

GOD'S SPIRIT-BREATH ACTS UPON INDIVIDUALS

WE have thus viewed the divine *ruah-spirit-breath* as a sign of God's gift of life throughout all of material creation. It is God's force by which he creates and sustains all of creation. Now we wish to see how God acts upon us by being the active source of knowledge, feeling, wisdom and other outstanding gifts, all bestowed by the Spirit so that we can contribute to God's over-all plan of salvation.

Job credits human understanding to God's breath. "But now I know that it is a breath in man, the inspiration of Shaddai, that gives discernment" (Jb 32:8). Even knowledge to accomplish works of art is attributed to God's Spirit as in the case of Bezalel's assignment to furnish the sanctuary (Ex 31:2 ff).

Both Joseph, the patriarch, and Daniel, the prophet, have the ability to interpret dreams because they possess the Spirit of God. Pharaoh asked his ministers: "Can we find any other man like this, possessing the spirit of God?" So Pharaoh said to Joseph, "Seeing that God has given you knowledge of all this, there can be no one so intelligent and wise as you" (Ex 41:38-39). Nebuchadnezzar acknowledges that Daniel is one "in whom the spirit of God Most Holy resides. . . ." (Dn 4:5).

Joshua is a man of wisdom in whom resides the *ruah* (Nb 27:18). He is "filled with the *ruah-spirit* of wisdom" (Dt 34:9). We must note that such knowledge is a gift of God's Spirit or presence working within an individual to produce a divinely desired effect.

Such in-filling of God's Spirit also is seen in God's gifting certain persons with extraordinary powers to accomplish feats of great strength or of leadership. Samson rips apart a lion (Jg 14:6), slays thirty men at Ashkelon (14:19), and slaughters a thousand men with an ass's jawbone (15:15).

The same Spirit of God infills the military leaders, Othniel (Jg 3:10), Gideon (6:34), Jephtah (11:29), and also Saul (1 S 11:6).

INSPIRATED PROPHETS

THE appearance of prophets filled with God's Spirit begins with Samuel. The typical prophet (called *nabi* in Hebrew, which probably means "one called by God to speak in his place"[7]) would often begin with some frenzied prophetic utterance. Samuel tells Saul: "You will meet a group of prophets . . . they will be in an ecstasy. Then the spirit of Yahweh will seize on you, and you will go into an ecstasy with them, and be changed into another man. . . ." (1 S 10:5-6). Such was the understanding of prophecy and the activity of

God's Spirit on a given prophet. It was a state of frenetic, wild, ecstatic possession attributed to God's Spirit.

Among the so-called classic prophets before the destruction of Jerusalem, the wild fury and ecstatic pronouncements are replaced with a different manifestation of God's Spirit. Such prophets as Amos, Hosea, Micah and early Isaiah attest that they are prophets, not because of some extraordinary, psycho-physical ecstatic behavior but because God had spoken his message, his *dabar* (word). Amos represents the classical prophets of this pre-exilic time when he says: "The lion roars: who can help feeling afraid? The Lord Yahweh speaks: who can refuse to prophesy?" (Am 3:8).

In the period of the Exile, we find the prophets appealing to the authenticity of their prophecies because it was the *ruah-spirit* of God, who inspired them to speak out his message to his people. The emphasis is placed on the direct, even physical impact of God's Spirit upon the prophet. In trito-Isaiah we find the prophets of the Exile personally aware of the Spirit's infilling: "The *ruah* of the Lord God is upon me, because the Lord has anointed me. . . ." (Is 61:1).

Often such exilic prophets added symbolic actions to attract attention through such a rhetorical device. Jeremiah bought the field at Anathoth to act out the prophecy that after the exile Yahweh would restore his people back to their lands in Judea. "For Yahweh Sabaoth, the God of Israel, says this: 'People will buy fields and vineyards in this land again' " (Jr 32:1-15).

THE SPIRIT OF THE FUTURE

THE last characteristic of true Jewish propheticism consists in presenting the Spirit of Yahweh as promising a new messianic kingdom. Ezekiel brings the consciousness of God's Spirit to the Jewish people to a new level. In his opening chapter, he challenges the Jews to live and trust in the world of the Spirit that cannot be only in past exploits, but also in a glorious future that lies beyond the imagination of the human person.

In his vision, Ezekiel saw the Spirit of God descending from the north upon Judea like a mighty storm (Ezk 1:4). The Spirit blew a cloud before it, out of which came four living creatures in the form of four men. These creatures went wherever the Spirit led them (1:12). However we might be prone to interpret all the amazing details of this vision, what remains inescapable can best be described in the words of the Swiss Scripture scholar, Eduard Schweizer:

> We might call it a world beyond the universe open to our
> exploration, but we must not take this in a spatial or
> geographical sense. Indeed this world of God is experienced
> by Ezekiel within his own earthly world. This means a life
> where God holds sway, a life beyond what we can normally
> see or recognize. At the same time the prophet sees that this
> world of infinity, hidden and mysterious though it is to us, is
> not sheer chaos, however chaotic the images may appear
> which force themselves upon our consciousness. It is replete
> with God's order; God's Spirit determines what is to happen
> there. [8]

The Spirit reveals a future ruler who will be completely filled with God's *ruah-spirit*, as described in Isaiah's well-known prophecy:

> A shoot springs from the stock of Jesse,
> a scion thrusts from his roots:
> on him the spirit of Yahweh rests,
> a spirit of wisdom and insight,
> a spirit of counsel and power,
> a spirit of knowledge and of the fear of Yahweh (Is 11:1-2).

This, combined with the familiar prophecy of Is 9:2-7, became the basis for the Messiah, the Anointed One, who would be full of the Spirit of God in an eminent way. "Here is my servant whom I uphold, my chosen one in whom my soul delights. I have endowed him with my spirit that he may bring true justice to the Nations" (Is 42:11).

This Servant will bring about a new exodus with Israel entering into the history of the world and its "nations" under his leadership, guided by the Spirit of Yahweh.

In the very familiar prophecies of Ezekiel 36 and 37, we see the future promise of a new heart given to Israel and a new Spirit put within it, a heart of flesh and no longer a heart of stone. The Spirit will breathe new life into the dry bones: "And I shall put my spirit in you, and you will live. . . ." (Ezk 37:14).

A UNIVERSAL SPIRIT

NOT only would Yahweh pour out the fullness of his Spirit upon the anointed Servant and also upon the House of Israel, but this same Spirit would be poured out universally over "all flesh." This prophecy would be fulfilled in the preaching of St. Peter on Pentecost when he links up Joel's prophecy with its beginning fulfillment in the outpouring in Jerusalem upon the first followers of Jesus:

> After this I will pour out my spirit on all mankind.
> Your sons and daughters shall prophesy.
> Your old men shall dream dreams,
> and your young men see visions.
> Even on the slaves, men and women,
> will I pour out my spirit in those days (Jl 2:28-29).

Here we see the Old Testament understanding of God's Spirit reaching its highest level of revelati n in the time of the classical prophets of the exilic period. The Spirit now is portrayed as the power of God who is lovingly concerned with building more than the House of Israel, but also a whole new world based on justice and peace for all men and women. But this cannot happen unless it begins to happen in the heart of each individual who accepts to be guided by the inner dwelling of God's Spirit. Only when our microcosm is Spirit-filled can we go forth in the Spirit's power to re-create a new world. The New Testament will witness in history that the fruit of the Spirit of God is love, joy and peace (Gal 5:22).

WISDOM AND GOD'S SPIRIT

BEFORE we close this chapter, we need to consider the Bible's sapiential literature and its relationship as wisdom to God's Spirit. We consider in the Old Testament, during the last four centuries befor the coming of the Lord, whole books of wisdom literature, such as Job and Proverbs (c. 450 B.C. and 200 B.C.), Qoheleth or Ecclesiastes, Sirach or Ecclesiasticus (c. 187 B.C.), numerous psalms and the book of Wisdom (c. 50 B.C.).

Jewish wisdom, although influenced by the sapiential literature of Egypt and other countries of the ancient Near East, always maintains a relation to faith in Yahweh who alone is truly wise, especially as shown in his creation. Gradually Wisdom appears as personified, being with God in his creation, reflecting attributes of divinity; and yet it is not identified with Yahweh nor is it a distinct created being. It is created from eternity.

Here we see Wisdom almost identified with God's Spirit, at least as the two of them are found together in God's actions toward his created world. Thus Wisdom shares with the Old Testament ideas of God's Spirit a close resemblance as a force or inner energy, with the power to transform individuals, nations, and the universe.

C. Larcher characterizes this intimate relationship between Wisdom and the Spirit:

> The two realities are identified in several ways. Wisdom possesses a spirit (Ws 7:22b). She also has power at her disposal and the various functions of the Spirit in the Old Testament are attributed to her. She has, for example, a universal cosmic function. She arouses the prophets. She acts as the great interior master of the souls of men. Wisdom and the Spirit are identified in so many respects that Wisdom appears above all as a sublimation of the part played by the Spirit in the Old Testament. This explains why some of the Fathers of the Church regarded Wisdom as prefiguring, not the Word, but the Holy Spirit. [9]

SUMMARY

WHEN we look back with the light of Christ revealing to us its inner meaning, on every page of the Old Testament we see the Holy Spirit as the loving presence of Yahweh. It is the creative force of God moving toward chaos and darkness and death and drawing the "void" into a sharing of God's being.

In Deuteronomy, the Spirit of God is depicted as a feminine presence, like a mother eagle, both protecting the weak and challenging the eaglets to greater life (Dt 32:11). The Spirit is God's *ruah*, a mighty wind stirring a static world into whirlwind movement, gentle breath of God imparting his own life into human beings (Gn 2:7).

God's Spirit was a protective cloud by day over the Israelites and a pillar of fire by night, lighting their way in the desert. He was the transforming power that, in the selecting of the judges and kings, challenged them to become true servants of God, teaching and ruling his people with justice and love. He was the "seeing voice" of such prophets as Isaiah, Jeremiah and Ezekiel, who foretold the messianic age through God's Spirit of universal love for all people and nations.

Human persons were to be given new hearts by God's Spirit (Ezk 36:26). This Spirit would transform barrenness into fertile land. "Once more there will be poured on us the Spirit from above; then shall the wilderness be fertile land and fertile land become forest" (Is 32:15).

God had prophesied through his chosen prophets that the living presence of his Spirit among his people would be poured out in a future age in great abundance (Jl 3:12-21).

The Spirit of God is, therefore, seen in the Old Testament as a loving presence of God, stirring his human children to a deeper relationship with him. That presence is never far away, yet it cannot be seen or controlled by us. It can only be experienced in surrendering love by those who search out that presence. "When you seek me you shall find me, when you seek me with all your heart" (Jr 29:13).

Now we turn to the Good News of the New Testament to discuss the full revelation of God's Spirit as the personalized love of the Father and the Son toward their creation in the incarnate Word. God's Spirit is not only distinct (as the Old Testament reveals) from our human spirit, but is shown to be one in nature with the Father and Son, and yet a distinct person from the other two.

St. Gregory Nazianzus in the 4th century was one of the great Greek mystical theologians who fought for the unique divine personhood of the Holy Spirit. Let me quote his belief in the Holy Spirit revealed to us in his fullness only through the

incarnate Word, Jesus Christ, but who has been indistinctly
traced in his unique personhood as God's gift of active love in
the Old Testament:

> For he [the Holy Spirit] is the Maker of all these, filling all
> with his essence, containing all things, filling the world in his
> essence, yet incapable of being comprehended in his power
> by the world; good, upright, princely by nature not by adop-
> tion; sanctifying, not sanctified; measuring, not measured;
> shared, not sharing; filling, not filled; containing, not con-
> tained; inherited, glorified, reckoned with the Father and the
> Son; held out as a threat; the finger of God; fire like God; to
> manifest, as I take it, his consubstantiality; the Creator-Spirit
> who by Baptism and by resurrection creates anew; the Spirit
> that knows all things, that teaches, that blows where and to
> what extent he wishes; that guides, talks, sends forth, sepa-
> rates, is angry or tempted; that reveals, illumines, quickens
> or rather is the very Light and Life; that makes temples, that
> deifies; that perfects so as even to anticipate Baptism, yet
> after Baptism to be sought as a separate gift; that does all
> things that God does . . . and making all things clear and
> plain; of independent power, unchangeable, almighty, all-
> seeing, penetrating all spirits that are intelligent, pure, most
> subtle.[10]

CHAPTER FIVE

The Holy Spirit In The New Testament

A SPARK OF LIGHTNING

WHEN the first disciples of Jesus gathered in the upper room, "joined in continuous prayer" (Ac 1:14), they must have felt of an excitement that shot through their group like a crackling spark of lightning on a hot summer night. Jesus had promised them ". . . but you will receive power when the Holy Spirit comes upon you, and then you will be my witnesses not only in Jerusalem but throughout Judea and Samaria, and indeed to the ends of the earth" (Ac 1:8).

Jesus had invited people, if they were open to his Spirit, to see in him what God looks like. They would be able to discover in Jesus God's hidden self-emptying love, the Holy Spirit, who acts in every human situation in loving power.

WHO SEES ME SEES MY SPIRIT

JESUS invited his disciples to see that he was the image or icon of the unseen Father (Col 1:15). "To have seen me is to have seen the Father" (Jn 14:9). He led people who heard him speak and saw him perform healings and miracles, into a world of mysterious experience of God's Love, God's Spirit that cannot be touched or captured by human ideas.

Jesus said little about the nature of God's Spirit, but he allowed the Spirit to saturate his every thought, word and deed. He could have said: "The Spirit is my image. It is my Spirit who will reveal to you who I am and what I have come to do in order to make you holy as I am holy."[1]

Only in Jesus do we know the Spirit as God's love in action toward us, and only in him can we receive his Spirit.

TWO WAYS OF STUDY

THE Spirit is Jesus' image. The only way to know the fullness of the Spirit's nature as God's loving activity toward us, and to receive the Spirit, is through God's communicating Word made flesh, Jesus Christ. A true christology brings us to a true pneumatology. Thus there are two ways of studying the Good News of God's gift of salvation to us, through his two hands, Jesus Christ and his Holy Spirit, in the words of St. Irenaeus.[2]

One way is to study the New Testament texts in their historical sequence as history that happened, beginning with the conception and birth of Jesus, his hidden and public life, his ministry of teaching and healing, his death and resurrection, the event of Pentecost upon the first Church and the mission to the world.

Another way is to study the literary sequence in which the books of the New Testament were written. We see for example the paradox that the earliest parts, Paul's epistles, were concerned with church problems rather than with historical events of the life of Jesus. They presuppose the oral tradition of the

Gospels, which deal with the earlier events of Jesus' history. Yet the actual writing of the Gospels takes place after Paul's writings. One of them, John's Gospel, is written toward the end of the first century.

STUDY OF THE GOSPELS

OUR knowledge, therefore, of Jesus, of his life, his actions and teachings, permeated by the Holy Spirit, comes primarily from the Gospel accounts.[4]

It is best to begin with the three Synoptic Gospels of Mark, Matthew and Luke, who deal with the historical account of Jesus' life. We will then move through Luke's Acts which give an historical account of the operations of the Holy Spirit within the early Church. We reserve to the end the writings of John and Paul that manifest a greater theological reflection on the nature and personality of the Holy Spirit.

In the New Testament, our knowledge of the Holy Spirit makes a quantum leap from what we find in the Old Testament. It is not a contradiction or a totally new revelation, but a more specific unfolding of what we have already seen in the previous chapter. Jesus came, not to destroy, but to fulfill what was revealed in the Old Testament (Mt 5:17).

This fact certainly applies to the fuller knowledge we receive of the Holy Spirit in the New Testament. The Spirit appears as "the Spirit of your Father (who) will be speaking in you" (Mt 20). He is "the Spirit of Jesus" (Ac 16:7); "the Spirit of life" (Rm 8:2); "the Spirit of sonship" (Rm 8:15); "the Spirit of grace" (Heb 10:29); "the Paraclete" (Jn 14:16).

The message of the Good News is that the Messiah has come and God's eternal plan of salvation is now being accomplished in Jesus Christ through his Spirit.

THE GOSPEL OF MARK

MARK opens his gospel by announcing: "The beginning of the Good News about Jesus Christ, the Son of God" (Mk 1:1). He starts his account at the beginning of Jesus' public ministry to show that now the power of the Spirit will be manifested in the teaching and healings of Jesus.

Mark begins with John the Baptist's call to repentance in the desert. Jesus receives baptism from John as an anointing of a *king, prophet,* and *servant* by the Spirit who comes to rest upon Jesus in the form of a dove, while the Father affirms in word his divine sonship.

The eschatological period, the beginning of the fulfillment of human salvation by the coming of the Holy Spirit, is announced. Jesus is singled out and consecrated as a prophet and savior. The Father gives Jesus his Spirit as the messianic gift, as the pledge (*arrha*) or first payment of the fulfillment to come at the end of the world.

THE HOLY SPIRIT AS A DOVE

ALL four evangelists describe the descent of the Holy Spirit as a dove upon Jesus at his baptism (Mk 1:10; Mt 3:16; Lk 3:22; Jn 1:33). Biblical scholars point out that doves were used as the sacrifice of the poor (Lk 2:25) in the Jewish temple rituals. We read in the Song of Songs that the dove was the sign of a new spring (Sg 2:11-14). Noah sent out a dove after the flood (Gn 8:8-12). This suggests the beginning of a new age through the symbol of the cleansing waters of baptism, here, by the anointing of Jesus by the Holy Spirit. We recall how the Spirit is depicted as a bird brooding over the waters (Gn 1:2), to bring out of chaos an ordered creation of new life.

George Montague well summarizes the symbolism of the dove in Jesus' baptism:

> Surely, then, the descent of the Holy Spirit as a dove over the waters is meant to suggest that a new creation and a new age is being introduced. For such was the meaning of the Spirit of God hovering over the primeval waters; and the waters of the flood indeed closed the old age and opened the new — and the dove was the herald of the new age begun. So too in Jesus emerging from the waters a new age and a new creation has begun.[6]

THE BELOVED SON OF THE FATHER

MARK, Matthew, and Luke also mention the voice that declares from above: "You are my Son, the Beloved, my favor rests on you" (Mk 1:11). This assumes an important role in relating their christology with their pneumatology. Paul could attest that our spirit and God's Spirit bear united witness that we are children of God and can cry out "Abba" (Rm 8:15-16). He could do this only because the faith of the early Christians was grounded on the natural sonship of Jesus from God, the eternal Father.

Mark wishes to show that in Jesus the Spirit of God and the prophetic word of God are now joined in fulfillment of the Scriptures. Jesus is not merely an adopted son. The Spirit's power in Jesus' works is a sign of his oneness in nature with the Father.

Mark relies on the prophecies of Isaiah to convey the sonship of Jesus to the Heavenly Father through his messianic role as Servant. "Here is my servant whom I uphold, my chosen one in whom my soul delights" (Is 42:1; see also Is 61:1). Yet for *servant*, Mark intentionally substitutes *Son*.

The rest of Mark's gospel will be a display of the Holy Spirit, working actively with divine power to show Jesus as *prophet, king, messiah,* and *true Son* of God.

JESUS IS TEMPTED IN THE DESERT

IN all three Synoptic Gospels we find the Spirit moving Jesus into the desert to confront the Devil. Mark dramatically uses the words ". . . the Spirit drove him out into the wilderness and he remained there for forty days, and was tempted by Satan" (Mk 1:12-13).

The Spirit drives Jesus in his public ministry to become the New Adam and to undo the work of the first Adam who yielded to the evil spirit. The Spirit anoints and actively drives Jesus into the desert in his own temptations (Heb 4:15) and in his exorcisms and healings as a sign that Jesus is bringing about the Kingdom of God through the Spirit (Mk 3:29).

Mark presents Jesus as the suffering Servant, whose fullest expression of God's self-emptying love only is manifested when he hangs on the cross, dying freely for love of all of us.

THE SPIRIT IN MATTHEW'S GOSPEL

MATTHEW wrote his gospel for Jewish converts to Christianity. He used Mark's gospel and a collection of Jesus' words and deeds which Luke also used, referred to by scholars as *Q* (for *Quelle,* German for Source) plus some original material not used by the other two synoptic writers. Thus Matthew has the account of the Spirit operating in Jesus' baptism and the temptations in the desert. With Luke he also has the Spirit working in the very conception of Jesus in the womb of Mary.

Matthew used his gospel to call his readers back to the basics, beyond the errors to which many of the Jewish converts were yielding. Thus Matthew highlights Jesus as fulfilling and surpassing the Law of the Old Testament.

Jesus is presented by Matthew as the beginner of a new race. He is a new Adam, the father of a messianic people. Abraham and David were the messianic forerunners who were types of a new nation more numerous than the sands of the seashore. Jesus comes as the completion, but even before Abraham was he exists. He becomes man through the cooperation of Mary and the Holy Spirit (Mt 1:20).

Like Mark and Luke, Matthew announces that Jesus is the one who directly leads disciples into the Kingdom of God. Matthew's audience and his scope must be kept in mind as we see a divinded church being called back to obedience under the visible authority Jesus gives directly from his Father to his apostles. The healings and exorcisms, the preaching and teaching of Jesus are the signs of the coming into fulfillment of the messianic kingdom long awaited by the Jews.

THE SPIRIT AND THE CHURCH

MATTHEW centers the attention of his readers upon Jesus and the words he gave them through the visible teaching authority in the Church. Jesus becomes the central discerning sign. "If the church has the Spirit, it is only because she has Jesus. Or, to put it another way, it is not because of the Spirit that she has Jesus (Luke's view) but because of Jesus that she has the Spirit."[8]

True discipleship for Matthew consists in observing all that Jesus had commanded (Mt 28:20). Ethical holiness in observing the two great commandments of love in obedience to the authority of Jesus, who continues his presence in his church through the teaching leaders, is the sign of a true disciple of Jesus.

LUKE'S GOSPEL

LUKE meant his gospel and the Acts of the Apostles which he authored to be complementary. The word *Spirit* occurs in Luke's gospel thirteen times and in the Acts forty-one times. He wished to aim his writings to the "gentile" world of Greek-speaking converts. Thus in the gospel Luke shows that Jesus alone possesses the Spirit, while in the Acts he shows the outpouring of the Spirit in explosive charismatic gifts of healing, teaching, witnessing to the risen Lord and, in general, bringing the Good News to all nations and peoples.

In Luke's gospel we are brought back to a parallelism with the Genesis account. The same loving presence of God, his Spirit, broods over the virgin earth, now Mary the virgin. "The Holy Spirit will come upon you and the power of the Most High will cover you with its shadow" (Lk 1:35). The Word of God becomes one with us within the womb of Mary through the activating presence of God's loving Spirit. Mary is full of grace and the Spirit inundates her, making her a fertile valley.

Here we see the full significance of the mystery of the active role of God's Spirit in the very act of Mary's conceiving God's Word made flesh. God's free, creative activity now comes to a peak of explosive love in the birth of Jesus. The giving of Jesus' name is most important: "You are to conceive and bear a son, and you must name him Jesus. He will be great and will be called son of the Most High. The Lord God will give him the throne of his ancestor David; he will rule over the House of Jacob for ever and his reign will have no end" (Lk 1:31-34).

The name of *Jesus*, in Hebrew and Aramaic, *Yeshua*, means "Yahweh is salvation."[9] Through Jesus, the Father brings liberation from sins and freedom in the Spirit to the world.

Luke shows that others possess the Holy Spirit as they play a role in the early life of Jesus. Elizabeth is brought by the Holy Spirit from sterility in her old age to fertility. Her child, John the Baptist, leaps with joy by the Spirit in her womb (Lk 1:41). Through the Spirit, Mary becomes the virgin mother of Christ. Zechariah, Elizabeth, Simeon and Anna, are all filled by the Spirit to praise and show joy at the beginning of a new age inaugurated by the birth of Jesus.

THE HOLY SPIRIT AND PRAYER

A unique characteristic of Luke's gospel is his association of the Holy Spirit and prayer. The Holy Spirit descends upon Jesus after he is baptized and stands aside in prayer (Lk 4:21). The disciples of Jesus were taught by him to pray to the Heavenly Father and he would give them the Holy Spirit (11:9-13). They watched Jesus pray early in the morning in deserted places or on mountain tops, absorbed through the Spirit in reverential self-surrender to the Father, and they learned from him how to pray in the Spirit.

Luke stresses the childlike trust and confidence (*parrhesia*) that followers of Jesus should have in asking the Father anything. It is the Spirit that fills Christians with such trust that alone drives away any fear and anxiety. "There is no need to be afraid, little flock, for it has pleased your Father to give you the kingdom" (12:32).

That same Spirit will give Christians the power to witness

before civil or religious authorities, "because when the
time comes, the Holy Spirit will teach you what you must
say" (12:12).

A GOSPEL OF MERCY

LUKE'S gospel is outstanding for its stress on God's mercy in
Jesus shown to the outcast, the broken and maimed, the
marginalized, the poor of the land. Mercy is God's infinite
love, coming down upon the miseries of his creatures to relieve
them and bring them into new life. Luke's gospel includes
many parables of Jesus for us to meditate on and through the
enlightenment of the Spirit discover God as a forgiving Father.

Typically representative are the three parables of God's
mercy: the lost sheep, the lost drachma, and the prodigal son
(15:1-32). Always when God's mercy and forgiveness are
accepted, Luke adds the note of rejoicing.

THE HOLY SPIRIT IN THE ACTS OF
THE APOSTLES

AS the Spirit came upon Jesus from the Father, so now in Acts
Luke shows us how the Spirit comes to Jesus' followers through
him. The activities of the Spirit are intrinsically bound up with
the risen Jesus Christ. Now we see the Spirit operating in
spectacular ways to foster deeper faith in the divine sonship of
Jesus. It is the powerful presence of the Holy Spirit which
assures the spread of the Church to all lands.

What are the special manifestations of the Spirit which we
find in Acts? The healings and exorcisms in Acts are not
specifically attributed to the Spirit, but done exclusively in the
name of Jesus. But the Spirit is manifested in the speaking in

tongues (Ac 2:4 ff; 10:46; 19:6); praising God (10:46); bold proclamation and witnessing to the risen Lord Jesus (2:11; 4:8; 4:31); power in confrontation before adversaries (6:10; 13:9) and, most prominent of all, new Christian prophecy that has been restored after prophecy ceased with the last of the canonical prophets, Haggai, Zechariah, and Malachi,[10] and vision (7:55) and guidance for the Church or for individuals (8:29; 10:19; 11:12; 13:2).

THE FIRST PENTECOST

THE Pentecost event is presented by Luke as an idealistic tableau of the community born as the People of Yahweh of the new covenant by the power of the Holy Spirit. It begins in Jerusalem after the resurrected Jesus is empowered by the Father to pour out the fullness of the Spirit upon his disciples to send them forth to proclaim to all nations "the mighty works of God."

The event is described in symbolic language. Pentecost means in Greek *fiftieth* and refers to the Jewish feast celebration seven weeks after the gathering of the first sheaf (Lv 23:15-16). Originally a harvest festival, it was later organized into one of the three great Jewish feasts that brought multitudes of pilgrims to Jerusalem. In the time of Jesus many Jews regarded it as a celebration of the giving of the Law to Moses on Mount Sinai, the inauguration of the covenant that made Israel God's chosen people.

Thus Luke draws together various elements from the Old Testament, all to point to the birth of a new people of Yahweh. The visible effects of wind and fire symbolize the coming upon the early Church-community of the Holy Spirit. The tongues of fire symbolize the power of the Spirit given to Jesus' followers to proclaim the Good News to the whole world.

THE FIRST CHRISTIAN SERMON

LUKE'S pneumatology can be found in his description of the external manifestations of the Spirit upon the disciples, in Peter's explanation of the events and their proper interpretation in the light of Jesus risen, and in their effects upon those baptized in order to receive the same Holy Spirit through repentance and forgiveness of their sins.

Peter explains the meaning of the descent of the Holy Spirit in the light of the Old Testament and then proclaims Christ as the Messiah, the Son of God. This discourse has been called "the most finished and polished specimen of the apostolic preaching, placed as it were in the shop window of the Jerusalem Church and of Luke's narrative."[11]

Peter quotes the prophecy of Joel to show that God has lived up to his promise made in the Old Testament:

> In the days to come — it is the Lord who speaks —
> I will pour out my spirit on all mankind.
> Their sons and daughters shall prophesy,
> your young men shall see visions,
> your old men shall dream dreams.
> Even on my slaves, men and women,
> in those days, I will pour out my spirit . . . (Ac 2:17-18).

In the second part of the sermon Peter gives a detailed interpretation of the Pentecost event as the culmination of the career of Jesus. He is presented as a prophet like Moses, authenticated by God. His death and resurrection were part of God's plan.

In the final section he discusses the resurrection as the fulfillment of two prophetic promises, Psalms 16:8-11 and 10:1. This is climaxed by the call for all Jews to acknowledge

Jesus as Lord and Messiah, who now has the power from the Father to bestow the Spirit upon all who wished to receive him.

PROMISE OF THE HOLY SPIRIT

BEFORE Jesus went to his death, a death he freely chose out of love for all human beings, he spoke of a baptism he would yet have to receive: "I have come to bring fire to the earth, and how I wish it were blazing already. There is a baptism I must still receive, and how great is my distress till it is over!" (Lk 12:49-50). It would be only after Jesus died on the cross that he could attain his new state of glory in which he could release the fullness of the Spirit upon his disciples. "John baptized with water but you, not many days from now, will be baptized with the Holy Spirit" (Ac 1:8).

At the end of Luke's gospel, Jesus tells his disciples: "And now I am sending down to you what the Father has promised. Stay in the city then, until you are clothed with the power on high" (Lk 24:49). At the beginning of Acts, Jesus tells his disciples not to leave Jerusalem, ". . . but to wait there for what the Father had promised" (Ac 1:4). Let us turn to the Acts to see the outpouring of the Spirit upon the Christian Church as the fulfillment of the Father's promise.

When some of the audience ask what must be done to receive the Spirit, Peter gives the essence of the evangelizing ministry of the early Christians: "You must repent and every one of you must be baptized in the name of Jesus Christ for the forgiveness of your sins, and you will receive the gift of the Holy Spirit" (2:38-39).

THE SPIRIT AND THE CHURCH

FROM Acts 3 through 28 we find a continuous historical account of the outpouring of the Holy Spirit through the mediation of the Church-community that moves out from Jerusalem to all parts of the then known world. We find no theological development of the "personality" of the Holy Spirit in Luke's Acts as we will find in the writings of John and Paul. What we find is a historical account of the signs and wonders effected through the gifts of the Holy Spirit to spread salvation and build up the Church. We find similar wonders of healing the sick and maimed as Jesus performed after he had received the over-shadowing of the Spirit in his baptism. But now the risen Jesus continues to do this through the church-members by the power of the Spirit.

Luke gives the history of the working of the Spirit in the Church's outward mission through the gifts of tongues and prophecy, healing, words of knowledge, wisdom, understanding, the power to witness before others that Jesus is Lord and Savior and to suffer persecution with joy.

THE WRITINGS OF JOHN

JOHN begins his gospel as the Old Testament begins: "In the beginning. . . ." But the Book of Genesis brought the reader to the first moment of creation. John leads us beyond that first moment back into the very heart of God as a community of love. God is pictured as "othering" himself as he begets himself and his Word from all eternity. The same presence of God as self-emptying love — depicted in Genesis as a Spirit that hovers over the chaos and the void — is hiddenly present as the bonding love between the Divine Mind and the Divine

Word. John would reveal in his gospel and first epistle his name as the Holy Spirit.

John the Baptist witnesses that he saw the Spirit like a dove rest upon Jesus (Jn 1:29-34). The Spirit flows out from Jesus to human beings, who open up in repentance to receive the Spirit. Jesus possesses the Spirit as an intimate oneness that is permanent. The language John the evangelist uses to describe the Spirit and his actions is used likewise to describe Jesus.[12] Thus John's christology is the basis for a similar pneumatology, since the Spirit flows out from the very inner core of Christ.

John's manner of presenting the Spirit radically differs from that of the Synoptic writers. An example of John's language, so rooted in symbols that lead the reader into the mysterious world of the transcendent and immanent Trinity, is Jesus' statement to Nicodemus: ". . . unless a man is born through water and the Spirit, he cannot enter the kingdom of God: what is born of the flesh is flesh; what is born of the Spirit is spirit" (Jn 3:5-6). This follows what John has written in his prologue of this new life, gratuitously given by the Father from above: "But to all who did accept him he gave power to become children of God, to all who believe in the name of him who was born not out of human stock or urge of the flesh or will of man but of God himself" (1:12-13).

This new birth by the Spirit is a true regeneration that goes beyond a mere adoption as a child of God. It is a true begetting of the Christian into God's very own life, by the grace of the Holy Spirit (Jn 1:13; 1 Jn 3:9; 5:1-18). God's seed abides in the Christian (1 Jn 3:9). This rebirth is the work of the Spirit.

LIVING WATER

JOHN, in narrating Jesus' encounter with the Samaritan woman at the well of Jacob (4:10-14), boldly uses the symbol of
living waters to refer to the Holy Spirit. Several Old Testament
texts associated water with God's Spirit (Gn 1:2; Is 32:15;
44:3). Jesus skillfully leads the Samaritan woman to desire a
water that will take away her thirst, namely the Holy Spirit.

John clearly identifies this water as the Holy Spirit that
Jesus would pour out (Jn 7:38-39). The text: "As Scripture
says: From his breast shall flow fountains of living water"
(7:38), is translated by scholars in two different ways. One,
generally accepted in Western Christianity, holds that "He
who believes in me will, as the Scripture has said, himself
become a fountain out of which streams of living water are
flowing forth." But the most ancient and traditional understanding of "from *his* breast shall flow fountains of living
water" stems from the Asia Minor churches and presents *Jesus*
as the one from whose breast shall flow fountains of living
water.

John the evangelist adds: "He was speaking of the Spirit
which those who believed in him were to receive; for there was
no Spirit as yet, because Jesus had not yet been glorified"
(7:39).

This is linked up with John's description of the pierced
side of Christ from which "immediately there came out blood
and water" (19:34).

Patristic writers, as Augustine, have commented on the
wounded side of Christ as the womb of Christ's heart, the image
of the love of the Father for all of his children, the Church, the
New Eve, drawn out of the New Adam.[13] Water and blood are
the symbols of the life-giving power that Jesus, dying on the
cross, gives to his Bride, the Church, in the birth-giving waters
of Baptism and the nourishing Body and Blood of Christ in the

Eucharist, both sacraments effected by the over-shadowing of the Holy Spirit.

THE PROMISE OF THE SPIRIT AS PARACLETE

IT is, however, in the so-called Last Supper Discourses that we learn more about the Holy Spirit in relationship with the Father and Jesus Christ and to the disciples and to the world. Such discourses, built around the promised gift of the Holy Spirit to Jesus' disciples after he had died on the cross and had risen from the dead laid the ground-work for the great mystical theologians of the 4th and 5th centuries who developed the trinitarian doctrine, the quintessential dogma of Christianity.

In the first text (Jn 14:15-18; 25-26), Jesus promises that he would ask the Father and he would give his disciples another Paraclete (from the Greek: *para-kalein*, meaning literally "to call to one's side"). The Paraclete "stands up" for us, interceding to "save" us (1 Jn 2:1). He is our helper, consoler, counselor. The disciples needed the assurance from Jesus that the gift of the Spirit would be another Paraclete or helper who would be continually dwelling within them.

We begin to see more specifically the nature of the Spirit by what he will do in the lives of the disciples. He will instruct them in everything and remind them of all Jesus had told them (14:26).

In the second text, Jesus assures the disciples that the Spirit of truth would bear witness on his behalf and would help them to witness him to the world (15:26-27).

In the third text (16:4-11), the Spirit would prosecute the world in the physical absence of Jesus and prove it wrong about "sin, justice and condemnation."

The prosecution of the world by the Spirit is unique to John's theology of the Spirit. It is the Spirit that will effect the conquest of all evil forces in the cosmos to bring about the eschatological judgment of God completing his plan of salvation.[14]

In the fourth text (16:12-15), the Spirit of truth will teach the disciples and raise them up as prophets to speak the truth to the world since the Spirit will be receiving all that belongs to the Father and the Son.

It is on Easter that John presents his version of the Pentecost event, by linking the outpouring of the Spirit as closely as possible with the glorification of Jesus. The disciples receive the Holy Spirit in order to exercise power in the new creation by receiving Jesus' authority to forgive sins (Jn 20:20-23).

RELATIONSHIPS OF THE PARACLETE

IN these discourses Jesus teaches us the intimate relationships of the Spirit with the Father, with the Son, with the disciples, and with the world.[15] Congar summarizes the nature, characteristics, and activities of the Holy Spirit in these discourses.[16]

The Spirit is of the truth; he is called the Holy Spirit. He dwells with the disciples and will be in them (14:17). He comes (16:17 ff; 16:13). He proceeds from the Father (15:26). He listens (16:3). He teaches (14:26). He makes known through communicating (16:13 ff). He reveals by speaking (16:13). He glorifies Jesus (16:14). He guides us into all the truth (16:13). He bears witness (15:26). He convicts the world of sin (16:8). He is given (14:16). He is sent (14:26; 15:26; 16:7). He is neither seen nor known (14:17). He is not received (14:17).

Under the power of the Spirit of the risen Jesus, the Church draws other truths to guide our lives according to Jesus

Christ, who is the Way, the Truth, and the Life (14:6). The Spirit is Jesus' image and reflects and reveals to us all we need to know about Jesus Christ and his Father. That is why John continually depicts the Holy Spirit as the Gift from both the Father and the Son to us, and through us to the world. The Spirit sanctifies and completes God's plan of salvation since the Spirit is ultimately God's Love as Gift poured into us and the world.

PAULINE WRITINGS

ONE of Paul's most original theological contributions to the early Church was his doctrine of the dynamic growth of the individual Christian, the Church, and the entire cosmos "in Christ" or "in the Spirit." There is for Paul a connection between the Spirit and the risen Jesus which is not something external, but internal and flowing out of their similar activities and natures. Thus for Paul to call us to live and walk in the Spirit (Gal 5:25) is to call us also to live "in Christ" (2 Cor 5:17). These terms in a special way are nearly interchangeable.

God's Spirit, by dwelling within us, makes us the temple of God's presence (1 Cor 3:16-17). As the Spirit of Christ, he makes us sons and daughters and we can cry out "Abba! Father!" (Gal 4:6).

Perhaps the best way to present Paul's doctrine on the Holy Spirit is to touch on the activities of the Holy Spirit in the life of the individual Christian, and also in the Church and in the world.

THE FLESH AND THE SPIRIT

PAUL uses the word *spirit* 146 times in his writings, 117 in his early epistles. One of his key concepts is his antithesis between the "flesh" and the "spirit." Flesh (in Greek *sarx*) represents for Paul ourselves in all our creaturehood in contrast to God, not only in our mortality and weakness, but also in our utter estrangement from God through sin.

This antithesis is developed mainly in Romans, chapter 7 and 8; 1 Corinthians, chapter 2 and 3, and Galatians, chapter 3 and 5. It is clearly presented in Philippians 3:3: "We are the real people of the circumcision, we who worship in accordance with the Spirit of God; we have our own glory from Christ Jesus without having to rely on a physical operation."

This is not merely a contrast between the inner, spiritual side of us and the outward, physical parts of our existence.[17] To live "according to the Spirit" means for Paul that a Christian is guided by the Holy Spirit on all body, soul, and spirit levels. This is to be attuned to God's holy will in every thought, word, and deed. It is to be a "new creation in Christ" (2 Cor 5:17).

THE SPIRIT OF SONSHIP

TO be spiritual is to experience, by the transforming power of the Holy Spirit of the risen Jesus, that we are really children of God and we can cry out "Abba! Father!" and know we are already co-heirs with Christ of eternal life (Rm 8:9-17). "Everyone moved by the Spirit is a son of God" (Rm 8:14). The Spirit frees us from the Law, bringing us into true freedom (2 Cor 3:17). The Holy Spirit brings forth his fruit in us that is: ". . . love, joy, peace, patience, kindness, goodness, trustfulness, gentleness and self-control" (Gal 5:22).

THE GIFTS OF THE SPIRIT

PAUL assigns to the Holy Spirit the character, initiative, and salvific action proper to an individual person. He had discovered through a personal experience "in the Spirit," the world of the Spirit. It was a "new sphere of life" (Rm 6:4) and the function of the Spirit was to create this new life in the risen Jesus. We have become alive by the Spirit so we must walk by the Spirit (Gal 5:16, 26).

Christians were *pneumatikoi,* spiritualized by the Spirit, because the primary function of the Spirit was recognized in the creation of this life in Christ. The possession of the Spirit was not the totality or the fullness of Christian perfection, but the Spirit was given as the "first fruits" (*arrabon*: pledge; 2 Cor 1:22, 5:5; Eph 1:14).

Absorbed with this new life in Christ, Paul moves easily between its manifestation on the level of the individual and that of the Christian community, the Church. He saw these levels as two points of view of the life of the risen Christ, living in both the individual and in the united members of his Body, the Church, with Christ as the head (Col 1:18).

Paul clearly exhorts the Corinthians to the ecclesial level of building up the Body of Christ through the gifts of the Spirit: "There is a variety of gifts but always the same Spirit; there are all sorts of service to be done, but always to the same Lord; working in all sorts of different ways in different people, it is the same God who is working in all of them" (1 Cor 12:4-7).

SPIRIT-DISCERNMENT

ONE of the important gifts of the Spirit in Paul's list of charisms given in 1 Cor 12:8 ff. is that of discernment of the workings of the true Spirit from those of the evil spirits. This he calls in Greek *diakrisis*, a judgment that sees through correctly from God's point of view. As Jesus taught, so does Paul, that it is the fruit produced by the Holy Spirit which determines whether any action is holy. Guidelines are found in Mt 7:15-23; 1 Cor 12:3; 1 Jn 4:1-6. This gift is a special knowledge given by the Spirit to build up the community of the Church through the greatest gift of the Spirit: love.

In his beautiful paean to true love, Paul gives us the ultimate discernment of Spirit-filled activities: without true love, all seeming gifts are nothing. Love alone will last forever (1 Cor 13 ff.).

PRAYING IN THE SPIRIT

WHEN we do not know how to pray as we ought, the Holy Spirit comes to help us in our weakness. The Spirit himself expresses our plea in a way that could never be put into words (Rm 8:26-27). This means more than singing in tongues. It is a non-verbal type of prayer that comes from the core of our being where the Spirit dwells and infuses his gifts of faith, hope, and love.

Paul exhorts the Thessalonians: "Be happy at all times; pray constantly; and for all things give thanks to God, because this is what God expects you to do in Christ Jesus" (1 Th 5:17). The Spirit gives us an inner perception of our dignity as children of God, filling us with freedom to dispose of our lives constantly according to the good pleasure of our Heavenly Father. He thus allows us to pray without ceasing through his gifts of faith, hope, and love, exercised by us in living situations.

RESURRECTION BY THE SPIRIT

FINALLY Paul holds out to us a sharing in the glory of the risen Jesus as we die to self: ". . .and if the Spirit of him who raised Jesus from the dead is living in you, then he who raised Jesus from the dead will give life to your own mortal bodies through his Spirit living in you" (Rm 8:11).

It is through the Spirit that God, who is love, communicates to us the power to be loving, filled with joy, abounding in patience, and, in general, putting on the mind of Christ in all thoughts, words, and deeds. The outpouring of the Spirit by the risen Jesus is the filling up in our hearts of the love of God (Rm 5:5). It is this Spirit who helps us to live in the resurrection and the victory of Jesus. We already share in the resurrectional life of Jesus through his Spirit.

> . . . when we were baptized we went into the tomb with him and joined him in death, so that as Christ was raised from death by the Father's glory, we too might live a new life (Rm 6:4)[18]

CHAPTER SIX

The Holy Spirit: God's Gift Of Love

THE CALL OF THE SPIRIT

GOD'S Spirit is calling us in each moment of our life to a sharing in the uncreated energies of the Father's infinite love that penetrate us at all times in his Son through their mutual Spirit of love.

The Holy Spirit calls us in loving service to build the world into a united community of peace and love. The Spirit never forces us to yield to his transforming presence. The gate that leads to this new love consciousness is small and the road narrow (Mt 7:14). The Spirit calls all human beings since God effectively desires that all persons attain the goal for which he has created them. But so few respond!

A NEW RELIGIOUS OUTLOOK

OUR concept of a detached God up in heaven, who cannot

have a real relationship with us, his creatures, has limited our view of God as a lovingly active Father, who is concerned with every aspect of our lives. He is not a far-away God, but he lives within us and is immanently present in all his creatures. He is the Orderer of the universe, inside of even the least sub-atomic particle, moving the world into greater consciousness and loving unity.

Our heavy rationalistic framework that has served to present Christianity to the West is in need of a complementary vision. Such a "new" vision is not really new. It is found in the Old and New Testaments, and in the Fathers of the Church. It is grounded more in perceptual, intuitive knowledge. It is an openness to God as mystery in which we meet the transcendent God in reverential awe and wonder. It takes our eyes away from ourselves and focuses our attention on a humble response to God's invitation to share his divine life through the communication of his Spirit of love.

SEARCH FOR A NEW SPIRITUALITY

WE have seen in the last two chapters on the Spirit working in the Old and New Testaments the immanent presence of God as a triune community of persons working dynamically through the unifying and sanctifying power of the Holy Spirit. If there is one Spirit at work in all of creation, there must be one spirituality that the Spirit evolves out of his loving activities among all human beings in relation to the Trinity, to Jesus Christ, to Christians, and to the entire world.

Yet the one Spirit, who works always toward bringing about greater unity in loving relationships, will allow for rich expressions of spiritualities. Still there is a basic triadic pattern in all true spiritual relations. This is manifested by "openness, actuation and growth."[1]

Jesus called his first disciples to "come and see," to that they would change as they learned from him through the Spirit's gift of faith (Mk 1:15). The first element in a new Christian spirituality is to have an openness to the breath of the Spirit, as he operates wherever and whenever he wishes. There can be no place in such a spirituality for "old wine skins," but only for "new" ones, so that they can be stretched by the new wine poured into them under the freshness of the movement of the Spirit.

This requires an effective new style of living out the inspirations and teachings of the Holy Spirit in a life of loving relationships of ourselves toward the Trinity, each other and the world around us. All of this must be under the dynamism of continued growth in greater consciousness through the infusion of the Spirit's faith, hope and love.

WHO IS THE HOLY SPIRIT?

OUR Christian faith assures us that God, as a trinitarian community of love, explodes in his self-emptying love to create a world of seemingly infinite diversity. Yet all multiplicity is essentially being guided by the loving, over-shadowing Holy Spirit to fashion a oneness, the fullness of the Logos-God enfleshed in matter. The Spirit is moving throughout the material world lovingly to draw God's embryonic creation into the definitive unity — the Body of Christ.

St. Athanasius in the 4th century expressed such Christian optimism in a world moving toward an ordered beauty and harmony through the Holy Spirit:

> Like a musician who has attuned his lyre, and by the artistic blending of low and high and medium tones produces a single melody, so the Wisdom of God, holding the universe like a lyre, adapting things heavenly to things earthly, and earthly

things to heavenly, harmonizes them all, and leading them by his will, makes one world and one world rder in beauty and harmony.[2]

THE SPIRIT AS A PRESENCE OF LOVE

GOD becomes actively present to us and invites us into intimate union with him through his Spirit of love. It is only God's love, his Spirit, who can bring about true communion in love. When God created woman and gave her to man, he breathed his Spirit of intimate love into them and bound them together into a union, bone of bone and flesh of flesh (Gn 2:23). Christianity guarantees that whenever we live in love toward each other, it is the Holy Spirit who perfects the love of God on earth, manifesting it in the material world (1 Jn 4:12).

We human beings seek communion in love with God and other human beings because God is this way in his very nature as Love. God the Father speaks his one, eternal Word through his Spirit of love. In that one Word, the Father is perfectly present, totally self-giving to his Son. But in his Spirit, the Father also hears his Word come back to him in a perfect, eternal "yes" of total surrendering Love, that is again the Holy Spirit.

THE FATHER'S PROMISE

BEFORE we can adequately study how the Holy Spirit indwells us, we need to consider him in his unique personhood, not only as he relates to the Father and Son, but especially as he is missioned to us by them.

The Spirit is spoken of in the New Testament, especially in John's Gospel, as being "sent" to us by Jesus Christ in his risen glory and power to transform us in an on-going union with the trinitarian community.

In Luke's Gospel Jesus, in his last instruction to his disciples, assures them that he would fulfill the Father's promise by sending upon them the Holy Spirit: "And now I am sending down to you what the Father has promised. Stay in the city then, until you are clothed with the power from on high" (Lk 24:49).

The Father had promised through the prophets, especially Ezekiel, that he would reveal himself to his people: "I shall never hide my face from them again, since I shall pour out my spirit on the House of Israel — it is the Lord Yahweh who speaks" (Ezk 39:29). The Father would be reflected in the image of his eternal Son made flesh, Jesus Christ (Col 1:1). Yet, as we already saw, the Spirit is called the image of Jesus Christ by Athanasius and the other Greek Fathers. Only through the Spirit can we truly believe and accept God's perfect gift of love manifested in Jesus Christ, but revealed as the Son of God by the gifts of the Spirit.[3]

Thus the fullness of God's love for his children can be discovered only when we receive the outpouring of the Holy Spirit. God had turned his face from the Jewish people because of their sins. But he promised to reveal his love by showing his face again to his people. "Now I am going to bring back the captives of Jacob, now I am going to take pity on the whole house of Israel and show myself jealous for my holy name" (Ezk 39:25).

The Gift of God whereby he would show his loving, merciful face to his people would be no exterior gift, but his very own Spirit, who would give them new life and a new heart:

> I shall pour clean water over you and you will be cleansed; I shall cleanse you of all your defilement and all your idols. I

shall give you a new heart, and put a new spirit in you; I shall remove the heart of stone from your bodies and give you a heart of flesh instead. I shall put my spirit in you and make you keep my laws and sincerely respect my observances. You will live in the land which I gave your ancestors. You shall be my people and I will be your God. I shall rescue you from all your defilement (Ezk 36:25-29).

This new Spirit is God's supreme Gift of tenderness and love that will be placed within the "heart" of each individual person who accepts this Gift. "I will give them a single heart and I will put a new spirit in them . . . so that they will keep my laws and respect my observances and put them into practice" (Ezk 11:19-20).

As we have seen earlier, in scriptural language, the human "heart" refers to the deepest core of all our human affectivity and freedom that determines our intentions and conduct. The Spirit is the Gift out of the "heart" of God the Father and Son who in their Gift of perfect love abide within us, if we live according to the promptings of the inner, indwelling Spirit.

ASK AND THE FATHER WILL GIVE YOU HIS SPIRIT

IN two parallel passages that speak of prayer in the New Testament, we see how the Spirit is the Father's greatest Gift. Matthew's Gospel describes the Heavenly Father as loving his children more than any earthly father could. As the latter would give only "good things" to his children, "how much more will your Father in heaven give good things to those who ask him" (Mt 7:11). In Luke's Gospel, instead of the phrase "good things," we find: ". . . how much more will the heavenly Father give the Holy Spirit to those who ask him" (Lk 11:13). The Holy Spirit is the best Gift of all "good things."

Even when we do not know what to pray for, the Spirit comes to our aid and prays to the Father on our behalf (Rm 8:26-27). The Spirit is the supreme Gift of the Father that embraces all other gifts, since the Spirit is the supreme, personalized Love of the Father and Son. The Spirit brings it about that we can become aware of the total Trinity dwelling within us because we have received this Gift of the Spirit: ". . . and this hope is not deceptive, because the love of God has been poured into our hearts by the Holy Spirit which has been given us" (Rm 5:5). In the next chapter we will discuss how this Spirit dwells within us.

THE FATHER GIVES HIMSELF TO US THROUGH HIS SPIRIT

THE Father promised in the Old Testament to gift us, his people, with his Spirit of love, through whom we can be transformed into new people, with "new hearts" to keep God's commandments to love him with our whole heart (Dt 6:6) and to love our neighbor as ourselves (Lv 19:18).

Jesus pledges his infallible word over and again in the New Testament that his Father will truly give us his Spirit. The Spirit images the Father's love for his children, and divinizes us into his sons and daughters.

When we receive this Spirit as Gift from the Father by faith (Gal 3:2, 14; Jn 7:38 ff.; Ac 11:17) and by baptism (1 Cor 6:11; Tt 3:5), the Spirit dwells with us (Rm 8:9; 1 Cor 3:16; 2 Tm 1:14), in our spirit (Rm 8:16; Rm 1:9) and even in our body (1 Cor 6:10).

THE SUPREME GIFT OF THE SON

THIS Spirit of the Father is also the Gift of the Son (Rm 8:9; Ph 1:19; Gal 4:6; Jn 14:26; 15:26; 16:7, 14). We are enabled to become truly sons and daughters of God our Father through Jesus, his only begotten Son (Rm 8:14-16; Gal 4:6 ff.). This Spirit acts ". . . so that Christ may live in your hearts through faith, and then, planted in love and built on love, you will with all the saints have strength to grasp the breadth and the length, the height and the depth; until, knowing the love of Christ, which is beyond all knowledge, you are filled with the utter fullness of God" (Eph 3:16-19).

Jesus is God the Father's gift of love: "Yes, God loved the world so much that he gave his only Son, so that everyone who believes in him may not be lost, but may have eternal life" (Jn 3:16). Yet it is through the Spirit of love that Jesus in his humanity becomes in his death-resurrection, the full, perfect image of the Father. Christ is risen from the dead by the power of the Holy Spirit. Because Jesus has the fullness of God's glory, he can send to us the fullness of the Spirit, who allows us to grow into greater glory through our oneness with the risen Lord Jesus.

CHRIST SENDS US HIS SPIRIT

TO the risen Christ, it has been given to bestow upon us the power and glory of God's Spirit. Jesus could not yet give the Spirit until he had died (Jn 7:39). But now Jesus sends us the fullness of God's Gift of love, the Spirit, who convinces us that the risen Lord lives within us: "We know that he lives in us by the Spirit that he has given us" (1 Jn 3:24).

By his victory over sin and death, Jesus is able to dwell within us and assure us that the Holy Spirit is the Father's definitive gift of love. The risen Jesus and the Holy Spirit cannot be separated, nor can the Father, since the Spirit is their mutual love dwelling within us as their supreme Gift to us.

Jesus had promised to send his disciples "another" Paraclete, an advocate, a consoler, a helper so they could live forever in their new oneness with the risen Lord that the Spirit would make possible. ". . . it is for your own good that I am going because unless I go, the Advocate will not come to you but if I do go, I will send him to you" (Jn 16:7). Jesus bade the disciples not to become saddened at his departure. "I will not leave you orphans; I will come back to you. In a short time the world will no longer see me; but you will see me, because I live and you will live" (Jn 14:16-19).

The coming of the Spirit will allow the disciples to know with faith, hope and love that Jesus would always dwell within them as the risen Lord. They need no longer be afraid, for he will be with them through the Gift of the Spirit unto the consummation of the world. Now Jesus' presence would be eternally living within the members of his Body, the Church, as the vine lives in the branches. "Make your home in me, as I make mine in you. . . . Whoever remains in me, with me in him, bears fruit in plenty" (Jn 15:4,5).

The Holy Spirit will bring to all Christian disciples this continual presence of the risen Jesus who transcends all history and yet is inserted into this world through the members of his Body, the Church.

THE SPIRIT MAKES CHRIST PRESENT TO US

THE Spirit does not only bring Jesus' risen presence to his disciples, who knew him in his lifetime. He is as well the Father's gift of eternal love to everyone who wishes to call Jesus Lord and Master through the same Spirit (1 Cor 12:4). The

Spirit, as the image of Christ, makes it possible for us to enter into an intimate friendship with Jesus that is more powerful, more everlasting than any such with him before he died. The Spirit makes Jesus present with all power and love. Through the Spirit we touch the same Jesus who walked this earth. We can hear him teach through the Spirit. Jesus risen still heals through the Spirit as he did on earth. The Spirit makes it possible for us to continually change our lives ". . . because you are from God and you have in you one who is greater than anyone in this world" (1 Jn 4:4).

We are never to be afraid or sad, but only rejoice: "You are sad now, but I shall see you again, and your hearts will be full of joy, and that joy no one shall take from you" (Jn 16:22). ". . . be brave: I have conquered the world" (Jn 16:33).

LOVE OF GOD IN PERSON

THE culmination of God's eternal plan of creation, of the incarnation and redemption of all human beings through Jesus Christ reaches its fullness in the Gift of the Holy Spirit to us. Here we reach the very mystery of God himself and the indwelling presence of the Trinity:

> These are the very things God has revealed to us through the Spirit, for the Spirit reaches the depths of everything, even the depths of God. After all, the depths of a man can only be known by his own spirit, not by any other man, and in the same way the depths of God can only be known by the Spirit of God (1 Cor 2:10-11).

The Spirit in his unique personhood is the very love and Gift of the other two persons of the Trinity. And we human

beings have been made in God's own image and likeness to live
in loving intimacy with the divine Trinity dwelling within us.
We have been made by God for love. We are called to establish
a communion of persons. Intimacy is thus at the heart of any
Christian spirituality. It is the primal work of the Spirit since it
is his very own nature as person to be self-emptying love.

God allows us to share his Spirit (1 Jn 4:13) and "as long
as we love one another God will live in us and his love will be
complete in us" (1 Jn 4:12). The Spirit makes it possible to
experience what E. E. Cummings wrote:

> it's not two ones are two
> but two are halves of one

In human love, there is nothing more noble than to
incarnate the mutual love of husband and wife in a living child
who will love forever and continually be the expression of that
love in an "othering" person. We see how the Spirit is not
merely a loving person, but is the personification of the love
between the Father and the Son for each other and for love of
us, his human children.

By divine inspiration God has given us in his scriptural
revelation two specific words to describe the Divine Gift of
Love. We read: "God is spirit" (Jn 4:24). All members of the
Trinity are equally spirit. But the Holy Spirit is aptly called
Spirit, which, as we have seen in Scripture, has the
characteristics of wind and breath. The Spirit is power, like the
wind. "The wind blows wherever it pleases; you hear its sound,
but you cannot tell where it comes from or where it is going.
That is how it is with all who are born of the Spirit" (Jn 3:8).

Love is strong as life, for no force can conquer love. It is
freely given as a gift that expresses the "donation" or giving of
one person to another in love. It is a joyful, spontaneous
outburst of self-giving. The Spirit is also likened to God's

breath: like love, it too comes out of the depths of God's very being to be given to God's creation. The Spirit is the Gift of the Father and the Son to their world, especially to us human beings.

The Father and the Son draw out from their very depths their mutual Spirit as life-giving love. They wish to en-spirit or breathe out the best in them as a Gift to others. This precious Gift of Love cannot be a creature but is an equal divine person, the Holy Spirit who transforms us into sharers of God's own nature (2 P 1:4), into children, loving in return God and neighbor. This Spirit permeates every part of our being. We become immersed in his living waters that cleanse us from all sin and death and invigorate us with God's very own life.

THE SPIRIT OF HOLINESS

THE Gift of God's Love, the Spirit, is also called in Scripture *holy*. As all three persons of the Trinity are spirit, so all three are holy. Yet the Holy Spirit is in a very special and unique way Holiness itself. All holiness in God is found in God's self-sacrificing love. But if the Spirit is Love, we should be able also to call the Spirit the Holy One.

In Scripture, whenever God is described as holy, he is always close to human beings or angels, involved in communicating his loving nature to others (cf. Lv 11:44-45). God's holiness is seen as he gives himself to us as a Gift of Love so we can truly participate in his very nature. Yet this loving union does not dissolve God and ourselves into one being.

Teilhard de Chardin gives us the pithy but powerful statement: "Love differentiates as it unites."[4] It is the Holy Spirit who brings about an ecstatic union that draws out at the same time the very uniqueness of the *I* and the *Thou* and the *We*. God's unique Love, the *We*, is the work of the Holy Spirit

(Eph 4:4). God does not give us primarily a "thing" or a created grace, but gives us himself as perfect love and perfect holiness. Thus we call God's personification of his self-giving love the Holy Spirit.

The Spirit of the risen Lord brings us into the holiness of the Trinity. Dwelling within us in deepest intimacy of total self-emptying love, God becomes present to us as holiness in his Spirit of love. Love brings communion, and in this intimate union with the indwelling Trinity we can be made holy to become "truly children of God" (1 Jn 3:1).

The Spirit is revealed in the joy of the Savior and his intimacy with the Father, all living intimately within us. Let us now turn our attention to the Spirit as the indwelling Gift of Love living in us as in his temple, and uniting us to the Father and Son.

CHAPTER SEVEN

The Holy Spirit Dwells Within You

THE TRINITY: GOD'S PERSONALIZED COMMUNITY OF LOVE

WE have seen in the preceding chapter how the Holy Spirit is the personalized gift of the Father and Son promised and sent by them into our hearts. Now we wish to explore in this chapter the mystery of the Holy Spirit as indwelling in the individual Christian. God's Spirit indwelling us makes us a "new creation." The Spirit not only works in us, but, miracle of miracles, he wishes to take up his abode within our hearts, at the core of our being.

We now have within us our personalized human nature, but also God's very own nature, which is to be active love through his Spirit. Two identities remain distinct without merging, yet they form a unity of loving persons present to each other that heightens the uniqueness of both.

THE SPIRIT DWELLS WITHIN US

IN the Spirit we discover the immense humility of the three divine persons of the Trinity who seek a union with us. The Spirit seeks to place himself in active, loving service by living within the limitations of our own human consciousness. Here the Spirit in self-emptying love serves to bring about the transformation of ourselves into regenerated children of God (Jn 3:3-5) unto eternal happiness by sharing with us God's very own nature. Within us the Spirit indwells as the most intimate presence of the Trinity toward us that it is possible for us to experience.

DEGREES OF GOD'S LOVING PRESENCE TO US

GOD is a community, therefore, of loving divine persons freely seeking to share their life with us. We are called by God's predilection (Eph 1:4) to an ever increasing consciousness of the Trinity dwelling within us. But the Gospel reveals to us that this is possible only through listening to the Word made flesh, Jesus Christ, who through his glorious resurrection sends the Holy Spirit into our hearts.

St. Paul beautifully describes this growth in awareness of the triune presence within us as the end of our human existence, the reason why God created us:

> Out of his infinite glory, may he give you the power through his Spirit for your hidden self to grow strong, so that Christ may live in your hearts through faith, and then, planted in love and built on love, you will with all the saints have strength to grasp the breadth and the length, the height and the depth; until, knowing the love of Christ, which is beyond all knowledge, you are filled with the utter fullness of God (Eph 3:16-19).

Let us now see how God reaches this most intimate indwelling within us by various degrees of unveiling to us his presence in all his creatures.

GOD AS CREATOR IS PRESENT IN ALL HIS CREATURES

IT is a central doctrine of creation as found in Scripture and the Church's teachings that God is near and immanently present in all his creatures. He has made (and is still in an on-going process making) this material world and conserves it in being by his immanent presence within each creature. God is everywhere immanently working inside as the primary cause and sustainer in being of all his creatures.

St. Thomas takes as his own Plato's statement: "The individual nature of a thing consists in the way it participates in the perfections of God" (*Summa Theologiae*, I, 14;6). Yet God is more present as he shares more of his perfections. We reflect more of God's beauty and goodness as he has created us to be sharers of his very own divine nature (1 P 1:4), by creating us "according to his own image and likeness" (Gn 1:26, 27). The higher a thing is in the scale of being, the more of God's perfections are manifested.

Bede Jarrett, O.P. describes God's presence as greater within us than in other creatures:

> The more life a thing has and the more freedom it acquires,
> then the nearer does it approach to God and the more divinity
> it holds. Man, by his intelligence, his deeper and richer life,
> his finer freedom, stands at the head of visible creation, and,
> in consequence, is more fully a shrine of God than lower
> forms of life. He bears a closer resemblance to the Divine
> intelligence and will and has a greater share in them.[1]

Thus we can conclude that, although God is completely everywhere in all his creation, yet he can be more fully present in us human beings than in other creatures. We should have great reverence toward God's creative presence in all creation, but especially toward every human being, including our own individual selves.

GOD'S PRESENCE TO HIS CHOSEN PEOPLE

ALTHOUGH Adam and Eve enjoyed a greater intimate presence with God than did other creatures — God communicated himself to them by walking with them in the coolness of the evening, speaking his word of self-giving love — our proto-parents sinned and broke away from God's presence. Still God was present as sustaining love to them. They ran away, out of their guilt and fear, as we find dramatically depicted in Gn 3:8, to escape God's loving presence.

Yet God re-established his intimate presence toward the human race by fashioning from among all the nations, a covenant-people. God chose one man, Abraham, to be the father of his people. Because he believed in God and obeyed him faithfully, he was justified, for to such God would again reveal his loving, intimate presence:

> I am El Shaddai. Bear yourself blameless in my presence, and I will make a covenant between myself and you, and increase your numbers greatly. . . . I will establish my covenant between myself and you, and your descendants after you, generation after generation a covenant in perpetuity, to be your God and the God of your descendants after you (Gn 17:2-8).

God speaks his Word from the burning bush that is not consumed. Such is the burning love of Yahweh for his children. He is a concerned Father revealing himself progressively in his actions done on behalf of his chosen people. He is a faithful, loving, protective presence among the oppressed, the poor, the broken and the humiliated. To those who need him and cry out, he will condescend and become present as healing love to them.

GOD IN THE DESERT

AS God fulfilled his promise to be a revealing presence of protective love among his people, he showed himself present in the luminous cloud. No one could look upon God and live (Ex 33:20). But he covered his Shekinah, his glory, so he could be with them, by the cloud by day and the pillar of fire by night, to guide and protect them (Ex 13:21-22).

Yet God wished to reveal his loving presence through his Word that he would speak in a concrete place. As long as the Israelites journeyed in the desert, Yahweh promised to "pitch" his tent among them. In that tent of the Tabernacle, God would speak to Moses "face to face, as a man speaks with his friend" (Ex 33:11).

In spite of their many disobediences, God's expressions of tender concern burst forth like meteors across the dark history calling his people back to his loving presence. "When you call to me, and come to plead with me, I will listen to you. When you seek me, you shall find me, when you seek me with all your heart" (Jr 29:12). God stoops down and picks up his child "like someone who lifts an infant close against his cheek" (Ho 11:4). And though a mother could forget her baby at the breast, "I will never forget you" (Is 49:15), promises Yahweh.

"But with everlasting love I have taken pity on you, your redeemer" (Is 54:7-8).

God dwells in the Ark of the Covenant. But he is more truly present in loving action in the poor and the humble, the widowed and orphaned. He who is awesome and absolute in his transcendence is one with the lowly in his tender, loving presence. He suffers with his people as he also rejoices with their fortune, their acceptance of himself as loving gift, eager almost with a holy impatience to be more intimately present to each of his children.

GOD PRESENT TO HIS PEOPLE IN HIS TEMPLE

WHEN Solomon built the beautiful Temple in Jerusalem as the focal point of God's loving presence among his people, he promised to communicate with them in a special way. The House of God sanctifies Jerusalem and makes her impregnable to all enemies (Ps 46:5-6; 48:2-4, 9).

Happiness in Jewish piety consists in dwelling near the place where God dwells in his Temple:

> How I love your palace,
>   Yahweh Sabaoth!
> How my soul yearns and pines
>   for Yahweh's courts!
> My heart and my flesh sing for joy
>   to the living God.
>
> A single day in your courts
>   is worth more than a thousand elsewhere;
> merely to stand on the steps of God's house
>   is better than living with the wicked (Ps 84:1-2, 4-5, 10).

To go into the Temple of Jerusalem and dwell there all the days of one's life, to gaze on Yahweh's holiness and loveliness in that blessed sanctuary becomes the cry, not only of the Psalmist, but of every believing Jew who could pilgrimage there on the great feasts. God's presence as communicating Word was felt powerfully in that holy dwelling place. All other presences of Yahweh among his people are summarized in this indwelling presence of God in the temple.[2]

GOD'S TEMPLE: JESUS CHRIST

THE central point in human history toward which all preceding events were leading, would be reached in the incarnation.

God speaks definitively his Word in the person, Jesus Christ. "Who hears me, hears the Father" is the sole authority for all his preaching and teaching. "Who sees me, sees the Father" is for God to pitch his tent and now dwell among us human beings (Jn 14:9). "He is the radiant light of God's glory and the perfect copy of his nature, sustaining the universe by his powerful command. . . ." (Heb 1:3).

The active Word of God, that was from the beginning creating new relationships with his people, now centers his presence in the "tent" of human flesh: ". . . and we saw his glory, the glory that is his as the only Son of the Father, full of grace and truth" (Jn 1:14).

GOD'S GLORY MADE FLESH

THE glory of God's divinity shone through the frailness and lowliness of Jesus' humanity. God's glory and power radiated in the teachings and miracles of this man Jesus. God's grace and life flowed through him. He touched people, looked upon them, loved them, spoke to them. His humanity is the focal point through which the life of God could flow into the lives of all who accepted him.

Jesus Christ is the New Law, the Torah. For as the Israelites received God's life and truth through the Jewish law given them by Moses, now life and truth have become incarnate in the person of Jesus Christ. He was the Light, yet the darkness strove to extinguish the Light. God had sent him as his saving presence among isolated and lonely people, starved for love. And yet "men have shown they prefer darkness to the light because their deeds were evil" (Jn 3:19). Those who receive Jesus as God's Light and loving presence into their hearts accept and live by the truth of Jesus' Spirit. Such live in the Light by doing all in God (Jn 3:21).

ABIDE IN ME AND I IN YOU

BEFORE his death, Jesus described his real baptism that would come about by God's Spirit working in him a love that would allow him to suffer and die, giving his last drop of water and blood for his disciples:

> I have come to bring fire to the earth, and how I wish it were blazing already! There is a baptism I must still receive, and how great is my distress till it is over! (Lk 12:49-50).

Jesus would be baptized on the cross in the Spirit of God's infinite love. His whole life was a movement under the guidance of the Spirit, but it was leading up to this "hour" of darkness. Out of that darkness Jesus would emerge into light, his glorious resurrectional life.

But before his death, Jesus could not give the fullness of the Spirit to his people (Jn 7:37-38). When Jesus was glorified "to the heights by God's right hand, he . . . received from the Father the Holy Spirit who was promised" (Ac 2:33). He could send the Spirit only after his death.

Jesus promised that he would ask the Father to send the Spirit of truth (Jn 15—29) to be with us, in the Church, and dwelling forever in each Christian. The Spirit would teach us everything and would bring to our consciousness everything that Jesus had said and done (Jn 14:25-27).

THE INDWELLING SPIRIT

ALTHOUGH Jesus in his humanity is the Way that leads us to the Father and sends us his Spirit, nevertheless the Spirit is God's indwelling love that reveals the presence of the Son with the Father abiding in us. For if the Spirit is indwelling within us, so also the inseparable Father and Son are one in their mutual presence as triune loving community.

Let us examine some of the main texts from St. Paul and St. John to see what the "indwelling" or "abiding" of the Spirit in us means.

Paul affirms the indwelling of the Spirit within the individual Christian as well as within the ecclesial community:

> Your interests, however, are not in the unspiritual, but in the spiritual, since the Spirit of God has made his home in you (*oikei en humin*). . . . In fact, unless you possessed the Spirit of Christ you would not belong to him . . . and if the Spirit of him who raised Jesus from the dead is living in you, then he who raised Jesus from the dead will give life to your own mortal bodies through his Spirit living in you (Rm 8:9-11).

> Didn't you realize that you were God's temple and that the Spirit of God was living among you (*oikei en humin*)? (1 Cor 3:16).

Your body, you know, is the temple of the Holy Spirit, who is
in you since you received him from God (1 Cor 6:19).

John seems to prefer, instead of the Greek *oikein*, to use
the term *menein*:

I shall ask the Father and he will give you another Advocate to
be with you for ever, that Spirit of truth . . .; you know him,
because he is with you, he is in you (*par 'humin menei kai en
humin estai*) (Jn 14:16-17).

. . . but as long as we love one another God will live in us (*en
hemin estin*) and his love will be complete in us. We can know
that we are living in him (*en auto menomen*) and he in us (*kai
autos en hemin*), because he has given us his Spirit (1 Jn
4:12-13).

Yves Congar prudently points out that the two Greek
terms, *oikein* and *menein* mean in general to *dwell, remain,
abide* in the Christian. The fundamental idea in both of these
words is that of a stable and intimate, affectionate relationship
between persons in an indestructible constancy. Congar cau-
tions us, however, that we are to derive the meaning from the
context.[3]

The Old Testament expresses God's physical nearness
and loving affection toward his people in two parallel streams:
that of his *hesed* covenant where Yahweh commits himself to an
everlasting, protective love toward his chosen people; and
that, later, of God's quasi-physical intimate presence within
the Holy of Holies (the inner sanctum) in the Temple in
Jerusalem.[4]

Paul and John build upon these two streams of Old
Testament thought, but also highlight a radical difference: the
Holy Spirit, as one with the Father and Son, effects for us

Christians the intimate relationship that the New Covenant brings about through Jesus Christ's resurrectional presence.

For Paul and John, the New Testament meaning of indwelling does not contradict the intimate union of the Old Testament Yahweh with his chosen people, but goes beyond it in a deeper union of love.

Luis M. Bermejo well describes the uniqueness of the New Testament understanding of the Holy Spirit's indwelling within the Christian:

> Furthermore, the Holy Spirit is far from being a remote person living in the inaccessible heavenly regions, behind the clouds and beyond reach. Far from it. On the contrary, the person of the Spirit *dwells within the sanctified Christian*, is continuously present in the most intimate recesses of his being. It is this astonishing, almost unbelievable proximity to man that goes under the name of indwelling. The Spirit breathes, lives and loves inside man. This is the wonder of baptismal sanctification. Not only has the glorified Christ given the Christian a share in his own personal life — the life he himself draws from the Father — but far better still, Christ makes the Holy Spirit live within the person of the Sanctified Christian.[5]

THE WORKING OF THE HOLY SPIRIT

IF the Holy Spirit is love and the Gift of the Father and the Son, it is proper that he is the one who indwells us since it is he who makes of us Christians a divine dwelling. The Spirit takes possession of our entire being. We are stamped by the "seal of the Holy Spirit of the Promise" (Eph 1:13). The Spirit regenerates us so that we are reborn by him (Jn 3:3, 5). He claims us in the name of the Trinity and makes us "God's children" (1 Jn 3:1).

The Spirit is the "pledge of our inheritance" (Eph 1:14).

By the graces he gives to us of faith, hope and love, the Spirit prepares for our openness to receive the Father and the Son. Jean Galot, S.J. explains this mystery of the indwelling Spirit as the first Gift of the Father and Son to us:

> His mission signifies that the Father and the Son wish to penetrate into us firstly as the pure love in order the better to penetrate us by their very own persons. At Pentecost, the Spirit descends upon the Christian community to allow Christ and the Father to come and dwell there.[6]

Entering into us, the Spirit brings to us the entire trinitarian family. The humble, self-effacing work of the Spirit, who penetrates into our very depths (1 Cor 2:11), does so only to bring us into an intimate sharing in the risen Jesus and the goodness of the Father, so that "God may be all in all" (1 Cor 15:28). He indwells us only in humble service to unite us to the Father and the Son and not to reflect glory upon himself.

The Spirit, sent by the Father as fruit of the redemption accomplished by Christ, makes the divine love to reside in us but in a way that the current of this love carries us to Christ and through him to the Father.

The Spirit exists within us to forget himself by being in his unique personhood the true love the Father and Son have for us. The Father, "the unoriginated Origin," in the words of Meister Eckhart, takes the initiative to communicate his gift of love through his Son, who manifests the emptying love of the Father for us in what we call our redemption.

The Father's full self-communication and communion with us is hidden in the human person of his Son made flesh. His full revelation is concentrated in the person of Jesus Christ (Jn 14:9; 15:9). Yet when Jesus assumed "the condition of a slave and became as men are; and being as all men are, he was humbler yet, even to accepting death, death on a cross"

(Ph 2:7-8), the Father raised him in the full glory of his resurrection.

Jesus Christ retires into hidden, self-emptying love by sending into our hearts the Spirit. It is the Spirit who exalts Jesus as Lord and Master of the universe (1 Cor 12:4; Col 1:15-20). It is the Holy Spirit who bears united witness with our spirits that we are the Father's children:

> Everyone moved by the Spirit is a son of God. The spirit you received is not the spirit of slaves bringing fear into your lives again; it is the spirit of sons, and it makes us cry out, "Abba, Father!" The Spirit himself and our spirit bear united witness that we are children of God. And if we are children we are heirs as well: heirs of God and coheirs with Christ, sharing his sufferings, so as to share his glory (Rm 8:14-17).

WE BELONG TO CHRIST

THE mediation of the Spirit indwelling in us only seeks to guide us toward Christ, the Way to the Heavenly Father. The intimacy of love the Spirit pours into our hearts (Rm 5:5) does not diminish our oneness with Jesus Christ. Rather the Spirit as the Father and Son's love for us unveils, bears witness to and expands this union.

The Spirit dwells within us in order that we can more consciously through his gifts of faith, hope and love realize that we belong to Jesus. "In fact, unless you possessed the Spirit of Christ you would not belong to him" (Rm 8:9). ". . . but the Advocate, the Holy Spirit, whom the Father will send in my name, will teach you everything and remind you of all I have said to you" (Jn 14:26).

Therefore, we see that the essence of the Spirit who proceeds from the Father and the Son is to lead us to the loving presence of the Father and Son in their self-emptying love for us. By abandoning ourselves to the guidance of the indwelling Spirit, we can be certain by the Spirit's faith that we are united through him to Jesus the Savior and our Heavenly Father, who abide through the Spirit in us as in their own temple.

RELATIONSHIP OF THE SPIRIT AND GRACE

WE will see in the next chapter the specific activities of the indwelling Spirit as he divinizes or sanctifies us. However, before we conclude this chapter on the Spirit's indwelling, we must reflect on the intimate relation of the Holy Spirit as uncreated Grace to the created gift of sanctifying grace.

CREATED AND UNCREATED GRACE

THE perennial problem in Christianity has always been: how does God, if he is perfect and immutable, communicate with us, his human children? Some theologians as Augustine and Thomas Aquinas over-emphasized the transcendence of God in his awesome perfection, and the unapproachableness on our part due to our sinfulness. The philosophies of Plato and Aristotle were used to explain that God communicated with us by created graces. The intimate personal relationships between the triune persons and the individual Christian were eclipsed along with the emphasis on the indwelling Spirit.

Grace for Thomas became a static "thing," which God would send down upon our souls. It is seen as an "entitative habit,"[7] the "originating principle of meritorious action by the intermediary action of the virtues."[8] A separation between our fallen nature and a superimposed supernatural grace becomes the habitual mode in which Thomas and most Catholic theologians until Vatican II conceived the concept of grace.

St. Thomas wrote: "Man needs a power added to his natural power by grace."[9] This Thomas calls grace, a thing which God bestows upon us human beings. Habitual grace justifies the soul or makes it acceptable to God. It is the infused, God-assisted habit of doing what God approves. Actual grace is the supernatural reality which God gives us as a means of assistance in doing good.

Grace, as Rahner writes against the static concept of grace coming out of medieval theology, is not a "created sanctifying 'quality' produced in a 'recipient' in a merely causal way by God."[10] Rahner comes very close to describing the uncreated energies in terms similar to the Eastern Christian Fathers when he writes:

> Each one of the three divine persons communicates himself to man in gratuitous grace in his own personal particularity and diversity. This trinitarian communication is the ontological ground of man's life in grace and eventually of the direct vision of the divine persons in eternity.[11]

As long a grace is conceived of as solely as created entity, all mystery and all inter-personal relationships between God and us are excluded. But more importantly, if we believe that God communicates himself to us merely through created graces, there would be no communication or gifting of himself to us. God would be a giver, not the gift itself. The Spirit would not truly indwell us as God's perfect self-emptying Gift of Love.[12]

We have already in Chapter One touched on God's uncreated energies. This is how more biblically and mystically oriented Eastern Fathers distinguished God's grace from his ineffable and incomprehensible essence that is truly immutable and unchanging. We can never totally communicate with God in his essence (Ex 33:23; 1 Jn 4:12; Jn 6:46). But the Good News Jesus has revealed to us through his Spirit is that the Trinity now abides within us and communicates to us unto the most intimate union of love through the divine "uncreated energies."

Such a distinction preserves the awesome transcendence of God and his trinitarian, personalized gifts of Father, Son and Spirit to us. The whole message of the Good News consists in God's revelation of himself as a loving Father, giving himself to us through his Son, Jesus Christ, in his Spirit. In that experience we can know God in his love-toward-us through his energies of love. These energies can never be conceived of as created "things," but rather as God, Father, Son and Holy Spirit, personally working in all events of our lives, to give themselves to us in loving union, brought about by the working of the Spirit of the risen Jesus.

God's energies of uncreated love are not God's action, but God himself is his action. It is the triune persons of the Father, uniquely different from the Son, both of them different from the unique Spirit, all working in gifting us Christians with themselves. These uncreated energies are not externalized gifts of God, but God giving himself to us in each divine person. They are called "uncreated" energies because their cause and origin is out of the essence of God who cannot be limited by time and space. His love endures forever.

Through these energies, God, as it were, goes beyond himself and becomes "transradiant" in order to communicate himself unto true union in self-giving to us.

CREATED GRACES

APPROACHING God through his uncreated energies, which

for the Eastern Fathers is "primary grace," does not rule out true created graces, called sanctifying and actual. The Holy Spirit is "the Spirit of grace" (Heb 10:29). As we shall point out in the next chapter, it is the Holy Spirit who sanctifies us. Yet our sanctification or divinization by grace is primarily effected by the indwelling Spirit, but also by the accompanying created grace which is inseparable from the Spirit. It is also never static or impersonal.

Thus grace is always discovered in inter-personal relationships; firstly within the Trinity in self-giving of each person to the others, and then in their giving themselves to us human persons. By God's free choice, we are created according to his own image and likeness (Gn 1:26-27) to have a natural inbuilt openness, not only toward other human beings in self-giving love, but above all and primarily toward the triune persons.

Deep in the core of our being where the Trinity dwells and continuously in their uncreated energies give themselves to us in love through the Holy Spirit, we can open up to receive God as *Grace*, as persons in self-giving gifts of each other to us. We can freely will to respond to this through the Holy Spirit's outpouring virtues of faith, hope and love. The Spirit then creates within us with our free cooperation a new relationship that is called created grace. It is a subjective disposition, a vital consciousness on our part that brings us to an intimate and personal relationship with the Trinity. This is both in the context of an affective and effective dialogue between the indwelling Trinity and the Christian through the Spirit.[13]

THE DYNAMISM OF GRACE

HOW can we describe the meaning of grace? We have seen that grace is primarily the Trinity's free, gratuitous self-giving to us whom God has called in Christ Jesus "to be holy and spotless, and to live through love in his presence" (Eph 1:4). Vladimir Lossky, the Russian Orthodox theologian, well expresses this:

> Grace . . . is the energy or procession of the one nature: the divinity insofar as it is ineffably distinct from the essence and communicates itself to created beings, deifying them.[14]

God's self-giving love confers upon us a condition that is completely beyond our own power to attain or hold on to. It is God the Father calling you and me to a "thou" relationship as his loving children. We are inserted into a real, vital and dynamic oneness with Jesus Christ as living members of his mystical Body, the Church. The Holy Spirit is the constant Gift of the outpouring love of the Father and Son toward us.

But we are called to respond to this dynamic, graceful relationship. We need to accept this awesome dignity to which God is calling us at all times, in all circumstances. Sanctifying grace is seen, therefore, as the work chiefly of the Spirit, who can never be personally separated from God's love given and our love returned to God's call.

We can understand, thus, how sanctifying grace can grow without any limits except what we humanly place on God's surrounding love. Peter Fransen well describes our personal cooperation in this graceful relationship toward the Trinity:

> Assenting to the persuasive urge of his presence, our heart unfolds and develops toward him. Free from self and already attached to God, *our fundamental option* made at baptism, grows steadily in firmness, assurance and strength . . . our "freedom of choice," which we exercise in daily actions, becomes more consistent, more consciously and deliberately directed to the task of life. Such is the normal pattern of

growth in virtue and holiness. The gradual process of bringing unity in the multiplicity of human activity goes steadily on under the gentle influence of the divine presence.[15]

AWARENESS OF GRACE

IF the Holy Spirit brings about within us the abiding presence of the Trinity, can we actually be aware of God as primacy grace, i.e., as uncreated energies of love? Can we be aware that we are truly responding to God's grace as self-gift of Father, Son and Holy Spirit? Can we truly know we are actively growing in sanctifying grace in our active responses given in our daily living? Can we be aware of the Spirit in his gift of sanctifying grace?

We have pointed out above that sanctifying grace is not an extrinsic, created quality. It is, in the words of Luis Bermejo: ". . . rather a new subjective disposition, a new attitude with regard to God that can best be described as an intimately personal relationship with him, an essential element in the affective and effective dialogue between the indwelling God and the believer who is indwelt."[16] The ideal model is of a Christian freely responding to the outpouring of the Spirit in his gifts of faith, hope and love, which cooperation itself is a part of the gift of sanctifying grace that comes from the indwelling Spirit.

DEGREES OF PRESENCE

A MOTHER and father are present to their baby. They are actively preparing by their daily presence as outpoured love in service toward the time when the child can respond freely as an adult by love returned to the parents. So the Holy Spirit in the case of a baptized infant is present and actively loving the baby to dispose it for the future relationship that the baby will evolve out of the indwelling presence of the Trinity.

But can adult Christians be consciously aware of the presence of grace in themselves? We might think that certain overwhelming religious experiences of ecstatic oneness with God might be an example of such awareness of grace. Yet here is where great discernment of the Holy Spirit and the fruit produced are so necessary and also so difficult.

Modern depth psychology shows us the intermeshing of vital forces from our various levels of body, psychic and spiritual activites. This should give us pause not to be too quick to attribute to the workings of the Holy Spirit all that we seemingly are aware of. If we make a daily examination of conscience, we can see how hard it is to arrive at the real motives impelling us to think, act or speak in a certain way.

That master-psychologist, St. Augustine, explains how we must show caution in trying to discern what was the real motivation in any given act or experience. In his *Confessions* he examines the use he has made of God's gift of the sense of smell and he discovers lamentable abysses deep down, even in his unconscious, that should make us hesitate to accept our own appraisal of our past actions:

> So it seems to me, though I may be deceiving myself, for there also is a lamentable darkness in which the capacities in me are hidden from myself, so that when my mind questions itself about its own powers it cannot be assured that its answers are to be believed. For what is in it is often hidden unless manifested by experience, and in this life, described as one continuous trial, no one ought to be oversure that, though it is capable of becoming better instead of worse, he is not actually becoming worse instead of better. But one can hope, our one confidence, our one firm promise is your mercy.[17]

INTERMESHING FORCES

WITH some honest introspection upon our past and present decisions, we discover a variety of impelling forces, some exerting more power upon our deliberation than others. At times we can see how such physical influences as sickness, physical dangers, natural calamities etc. inhibit our free deliberation.

In the spiritual realm we all continually experience the hidden forces of evil: "Be calm, but vigilant because your enemy the devil is prowling around like a roaring lion, looking for someone to eat" (1 P 5:8-9). It is often impossible for us to arrive at a right appraisal of our moral conduct. Our awareness of our inner motivation can never be one of perfect rational clarity and certainty.

Yet God's Spirit of love dwells deeply inside the "core" of our being, even within our unconscious. The Holy Spirit is our source of strength and right-living, and is working to heal, transform and direct us "home" to a more intimate, loving oneness with the indwelling Trinity. We do not have an immediate, perfectly clear awareness of this except through faith, hope and love, as in this life we always are "seeing a dim reflection in a mirror" (1 Cor 13:12).

It is with childlike humility that we open up to the Spirit's gentle, creative love. Grace never forces us to act in this or that fixed manner. Grace "allures" us by the attraction of a delicate yet strong presence through faith, calling us from the depths of our being to come home to our loving Father. The Good News is that the Father is grace, uncreated love, always present within us and around us and acting in a self-emptying gifting of himself to us in the Son through the indwelling Spirit.

GRACE: A DIALOGUE OF LOVING COOPERATION

THE continued invitations to us from the Spirit are created graces that call us to respond. When, in our infirmities, brokenness, fears, doubts and even sinfulness, we freely will to answer this invitation in faith, trust and love, we can call this relationship *sanctifying grace*. We freely co-operate, yet even our response is covered with God's enticing love, the Holy Spirit. Without the work of the Spirit, we would be unable to be saved, healed, transformed into children of the Heavenly Father.

We truly are the result of the Spirit's grace. Yet, like Mary, the Mother of Jesus, we too can receive the greeting of the angel Gabriel: "Rejoice, so highly favored. The Lord is with you" (Lk 1:28-29). All is grace that comes from God's personified Love, the Holy Spirit! Yet to be sanctified and made holy as our Heavenly Father is holy, we need to respond. We can destroy the dialogue of loving mutually and thus break the living presence of sanctifying grace that binds us through the Spirit in loving union with the Trinity. The Trinity can never be driven away. But we can freely say no to the Spirit, stifle his invitation and shut ourselves off from sanctifying grace, which makes possible our loving cooperation with the Holy Spirit.

Let us now see how the Holy Spirit sanctifies us and how we are to cooperate by responding freely to God's enticing graces.

CHAPTER EIGHT

The Holy Spirit Sanctifies Us

CALLED TO BE HOLY

GOD alone is holy, but he calls us to be holy as he is holy. We need to cooperate, but it is ultimately only the Father who makes us holy in and through the incarnate Son, Jesus Christ, and his Spirit. ". . . but now you have been washed clean, and sancfitied, and justified through the name of the Lord Jesus Christ and through the Spirit of our God" (1 Cor 6:11). ". . . God chose you from the beginning to be saved by the sanctified Spirit and by faith in the truth" (2 Th 2:13).

Christianity presents us with some fundamental truths which call us to respond and live our lives according to them. This is why the early Eastern Fathers have always insisted that *orthodoxia*, right teaching, as reveald to us by God, must impact our lives and lead us to *orthopraxis*, or right living according to such truths.

We have seen in the last chapter the sublime truth that

the Spirit dwells within us and is the love binding us to the abiding presence of the Father and the Son. Such a revealed truth must be experienced in faith and lived in hope and love. Let us now see how the indwelling Holy Spirit divinizes us into holy and loving children of the all-holy Father. We are to grow continually by the sanctifying power of the Holy Spirit to be holy children of God.

Two hymns sung at Vespers in the Byzantine Churches on Monday of Pentecost well summarize the work of the Holy Spirit:

> The Holy Spirit always was and always shall be, for he is with the Father and the Son, one of the Trinity. He is both life and life-giving. He is light, and by nature, the giver of light. He is all-holy and the source of holiness. Through him, we know the Father and glorify the Son, understanding that the Holy Trinity is a single power, three of equal rank and equally to be worshiped.

> The Holy Spirit is light and life, a living fountain of all spiritual reality. He is the essence of wisdom, the Spirit of knowledge. He is goodness and understanding, the leader of righteousness. He cleanses us from sin. He is divine and makes us so. He is fire proceeding from fire. His word is action, the distribution of gifts. Through Him God's witnesses, prophets and apostles were crowned. Oh, the marvel of this truth! Oh, the marvel of this sight: Tongues of fire bringing about the distribution of gifts![1]

GOD IS HOLY

THE Holy Spirit is the sanctifying power of the Trinity. Sanctity according to St. Cyril of Alexandria is as essential to the

Holy Spirit as paternity is to the Father and filiation to the Son.[2] Cyril writes:

> If the Holy Spirit does not work through himself in us, if he is not by nature that which we know, if, after having been filled by the divine essence of a participated sanctification, he could only commune to us a grace which had been given to him, it is evident that it is through a creature that the grace of the Holy Spirit is administered to us. But this is not so. . . . The Holy Spirit works through himself in us, sanctifying us and uniting us to himself.[3]

In the First Epistle of Peter our human goal is revealed to us: ". . . be holy in all you do, since it is the Holy One who has called you; and Scripture says: 'Be holy, for I am holy' " (1 P 1:15-16). What does it mean to say God is holy? In Scripture, whenever God is described as holy, he is always close to human beings or angels, involved in communicating his loving nature so that his perfections can be shared in a union of love.

> For it is I, Yahweh, who are your God. You have been sanctified and have become holy because I am holy. . . . Yes, it is I, Yahweh, who have brought you out of Egypt to be your God; you, therefore, must be holy because I am holy (Lv 11:44-45).

God is holy because he freely and gratuitously wishes to share the fullness of his being with us. God is a community of self-emptying love of three persons in a unity of love in order that we might share for all eternity in their goodness and beauty. God freely seeks actively to create with us a loving community, a *koinonia* or fellowship in the Spirit of love, so that we can truly participate in his very nature. Yet, this union does not dissolve God and ourselves into a unity without uniqueness or distinction.

Christianity insists on the oneness of creatures in God, but holiness preserves also the otherness of God, which permits true and even passionate love on the part of God toward his human children. Holiness is the special way God's graciousness and perfect freedom come to us through his specifically unique and constant energies of love. Holiness adds a most important dimension to God's essence, not presented in the concept of God as grace. That is, that God in being true to his divine nature as love, must also judge and abhor anything that resists and opposes himself as grace. God's holiness necessitates that God's will must always prevail, and this necessitates judgment on what resists God's free love.[4]

THE SANCTIFYING HOLY SPIRIT

IT is we who have to become "perfect" as our Heavenly Father is perfect (Mt 5:48), to become "holy" as he is holy. The Holy Spirit anointed Jesus in his humanity and gave him the power to be holy, self-emptying in loving obedience to his Heavenly Father in each moment of his earthly existence just as the Father was holy in self-giving love to Jesus. The same Holy Spirit brings us his sanctifying power, making it possible with our cooperation to become truly holy as Jesus and the Father are holy.

The Spirit overwhelms us by God's holiness, and we eagerly wish to obey the Divine Word, enfleshed for love of us to image God's holiness, as he directs us from within through his Holy Spirit.

We enter into God's holiness in our own heart. We now have the right to go "into the sanctuary" by the blood of Jesus, our high priest. We now have the power through the Spirit to become holy as God is holy. It is not by our power or our works that we become holy. It is in Jesus, our powerful high priest, who intercedes for us that the Father will release his Spirit, who will reveal to us that we now live intimately in God's self-emptying holiness. One with Christ, we are one with the Trinity, Father, Son and Holy Spirit. We can now do all as a symbol of the return of ourselves totally to God as gift. We are possessed totally by God. We burn with passion still more to live only in Christ and no longer for ourselves (Gal 2:20).

Humbled by God's holiness revealed in Jesus Christ, we joyfully seek to respond by living lives of Christlike holiness. "We are God's work of art, created in Christ Jesus to live the good life as from the beginning he had meant for us to live it" (Eph 2:10).

THE SPIRIT UNITES US TO CHRIST

THE first work in the Spirit's sanctifying us is to reveal to us the Good News of God's great love for us in giving us his only begotten Son that we might have eternal life (Jn 3:16). The New Testament shows us how the Spirit reveals the presence of Christ and makes us know him as our Savior, the true Son of God from all eternity who has freely become human to die for us that we might experience this constant, eternal love of the Trinity though Jesus' abiding oneness with us.

In Scripture we see the Holy Spirit always preparing the way for people to accept Jesus as the Messiah, the Savior of the world. Paul writes: ". . . no one can say, 'Jesus is Lord' unless he is under the influence of the Holy Spirit" (1 Cor 12:3). In the Old Testament, the Spirit illumines the prophets to give the people the outline of the Messiah's traits so when he would come, they would recognize him as the Father's ambassador, the Savior and Anointed One.

The Spirit made Elizabeth recognize Jesus in Mary's

womb (Lk 1:41-43). Simeon in the temple was guided by the Spirit to recognize the long-awaited Savior in Mary's child (Lk 2:25-27). So also in our hearts the Spirit orients toward Jesus as the Divine Savior. The Spirit, as Jesus promised, would be his gift and that of the Father who would be with us and in us always (Jn 14:17). He would teach us everything and remind us of all he had said (Jn 14:26).

The Holy Spirit would be Jesus' witness to us and make us his witnesses to the world (Jn 15:26-27). He will lead us to the complete truth and he will glorify Jesus (Jn 16:13). The Holy Spirit enkindles his fire of divine love within our hearts so that we can surrender our lives entirely to the guidance of Jesus Christ.

DISCOVERING JESUS AS THE LIVING WORD

OUR journey toward holiness begins by the Spirit bringing us into the living presence of the risen Lord Jesus by unveiling his active presence in us through the Word in Scripture. The Spirit inspires us to understand Scripture since he is the divine author. The Holy Spirit even in the Old Testament was always pointing to the full manifestation of God's *hesed* covenant to be completed in Jesus, the New Covenant. The Spirit guides our interpretation as he unveils hidden meanings which he allows to be discovered through the Church by the Christian community.

The Spirit safeguards the teaching authority of the Church to guide us with inerrancy. The Spirit reveals the attitudes of Jesus toward the Heavenly Father and the world, and makes us witnesses in our contemporary times to the eternal values revealed by Christ.

UNION WITH JESUS

ESSENTIAL to our process of becoming holy as God is holy is to allow the Holy Spirit to ground us in faith and love of Jesus Christ by plunging us into the knowledge of him that surpasses all understanding (Eph 3:16). We must know Jesus if we are to love him and be guided by his inner direction of us in every thought, word and deed. "We know that he [Jesus] lives in us by the Spirit that he has given us" (1 Jn 3:24).

The Spirit helps us to know Jesus more intimately and love him more ardently. The Spirit provides the grace for us to be more and more fascinated by Christ. Paul witnesses to the great personal love he has for Jesus:

> I have been crucified with Christ, and I live now not with my own life but with the life of Christ who lives in me. The life I now live in this body I live in faith: faith in the Son of God who loved me and who sacrificed himself for my sake (Gal 2:19-20).

JESUS: THE SUFFERING SERVANT

THE Spirit leads us to see in the crucified suffering-servant, Jesus, God's love fully revealed. "Who sees me sees the Father" (Jn 14:9). Our sanctification begins by our experiencing Jesus as truly God and truly man who freely dies for love of us. Jesus preached about the Kingdom of God, of the Father's great love for his children. But he came also as a perfect image of the Father's love.

The good news was not only that God was a loving Father of infinite mercy, but that the "in-breaking" of God's energies of love into human lives was being effected by the man, Jesus of Nazareth. It was not so much his preaching that burst the bonds that held the human race in slavery but it was he himself, the Word, that was the liberating power (Jn 8:31-32).

The Spirit gives to us a new wisdom that contradicts the wise ones of this world. "The hidden wisdom of God which we preach in our mysteries is the wisdom that God predestined to be for our glory before the ages began. It is a wisdom that none of the masters of this age have ever known, or they would not have crucified the Lord of Glory. We teach what Scripture calls: the things that no eye has seen and no ear has heard, things beyond the mind of man, all that God has prepared for those who love him" (1 Cor 2:7-9).

Pentecost with the outpouring of the Spirit brings about a return to Calvary and the cross. This new wisdom gives us the courage to respond to Jesus and live a life of similar self-emptying love in his Body.

The Spirit creates the intimacy of friend to friend between Jesus and the Christian, making it possible for us to bring under captivity and in obedience to Jesus every thought and every imagination (2 Cor 10:5). The Spirit thus helps us by his grace to embrace sufferings that come from loving God with our whole heart and loving our neighbor as we love ourselves.

He inspires in us the inner disciplines of recollection, humility, self-abnegation, zeal for others, repentance and love for God and neighbor. The Spirit gives us unique, individual inspirations. The Spirit does not lead everyone by the same path, but inspires each Christian differently in such areas as apostolic zeal, penance, prayer, and fraternal charity. Love is proved by deeds, but each person responds freely to the movement of the Holy Spirit to return the love of the Father as manifested to us by Jesus Christ. This is where, as we will point out in discussing spiritual discernment, there is a need for spiritual guidance.

CHILDREN OF THE HEAVENLY FATHER

THE early Eastern Fathers, from Irenaeus on, tell us why God became incarnated: God became man in order that man might become God.[5] The Holy Spirit brings us into ultimate intimacy through Christ, the only begotten Son, who shares with us his divine sonship with the Father.

The main work of the Holy Spirit is to bring about in us a new birth, a new regeneration whereby we can share in the filiation of the only begotten Son of God. Jesus had told Nicodemus of the necessity of being reborn of water and the Spirit (Jn 3:5-6). And Paul often described the chief work of the Spirit as bringing us into a new life, a life in Jesus, which regenerates us into children of God:

> . . . the Spirit of God has made his home in you. . . . Though your body may be dead it is because of sin, but if Christ is in you then your spirit is life itself because you have been justified, and if the Spirit of him who raised Jesus from the dead is living in you, then he who raised Jesus from the dead will give life to your own mortal bodies through his Spirit living in you (Rm 8:9-11).

RAISED TO A NEW DIGNITY

BECAUSE the Spirit of Jesus is given to us by the love of God that abounds in us (Rm 5:5), we are made from slaves to be now children of God. "The Spirit himself and our spirit bear united witness that we are children of God. And if we are children we are heirs as well: heirs of God and co-heirs with Christ, sharing his suffering so as to share his glory" (Rm 8:16-17; also Gal 4:6).

We are thus able to share in Jesus' very own life because of his Spirit that he gives us. As we strive to live by the Holy Spirit according to this inner dignity, we become "God's children and that is what we really are" (1 Jn 3:1). We are called out of darkness into the light of Jesus risen and therefore we must put aside the works of darkness.

Paul appeals to this inner dignity when he describes our physical bodies as temples of God:

> Didn't you realize that you were God's temple and that the Spirit of God was living among you? If anybody should destroy the temple of God, God will destroy him, because the temple of God is sacred and you are that temple (1 Cor 3:16; cf. 1 Cor 6:12).

Paul assigns to the Holy Spirit the character, initiative and salvific action proper to a person. "Since the Spirit is our life, let us be directed by the Spirit" (Gal 5:25).

CHRISTIANS BECOME SPIRIT-BEARERS

CHRISTIANS are of the Spirit, *pneumatikoi* in Greek. We are spiritualized by the Spirit because his primary function is recognized in the creation of this new life in Christ Jesus. The Spirit is given as the "first-fruits" of Christian perfection (Rm 8:23) and the pledge or guarantee of its completion (2 Cor 1:22; Eph 1:14). The phrases, "in the Spirit" and "in Christ," for Paul are complementary to each other. The Spirit who was the love-power bringing about the birth of the Son of God in human form also brings forth divine life within us Christians. He does this if we cooperate to live according to this inner power of the Spirit, who reveals the mind of Christ and empowers us to respond and progress into a greater likeness to Jesus.

TWO FORCES

PAUL sees Christians as caught within the dialectic of two forces: the power of evil and the Spirit of Jesus. They must live according to the Spirit which creates the new life of Christ within them. He also fosters and brings it to its fullness by guiding us to make choices in accord with the living Word-incarnate.

Ideally our life is freed from any extrinsic law and is guided by an interior communication that we receive when we turn within and listen to the Spirit of Jesus. "If you are led by the Spirit, no law can touch you" (Gal 5:18). Christians are known by the evident fruit of the Spirit that accompanies their choices:

> What the Spirit brings is very different: love, joy, peace, patience, kindness, goodness, trustfulness, gentleness and self-control. There can be no law against things like that, of course. . . . Since the Spirit is our life, let us be directed by the Spirit (Gal 5:22-25).

The Spirit guides us to respond constantly to the living Word within. He reveals to us God's will through the Church. He allows us to participate in the Holy Eucharist. These are the works of the Holy Spirit in individual Christians to bring them to respond to the living Word along with the unifying, loving force of the Spirit within the Church and to union with one another in the Eucharist.

THE CROSS AND RESURRECTION

THE Spirit of Jesus reveals to us how we are to always try to please God, to lead "a life acceptable to him in all its aspects"

(Col 1:10). But this cannot be done unless we are ready to put to death our carnal desires and put on the mind of Christ. The Spirit comes to help us in our weakness (Rm 8:26). He prays in us when we do not know how to pray.

But above all, the Spirit fills us with the inner law of charity. It is by the Spirit's love infused into us that we can live according to the mind of Jesus. Through the love of God poured into our hearts we can be always patient and kind, never jealous, or boastful or conceited or rude or selfish. We need no more to take offense or be resentful. We will always be ready to excuse, to trust, to hope and to endure whatever comes. For love is the greatest gift of God. It is truly the Holy Spirit himself operating freely withn us (1 Cor 13:4-13).

DIVINIZATION

IN Eastern theology the teaching of *theosis* or divinization is the theological "locus" or place in which the work of the Holy Spirit in our regard is highlighted. Divinization is the continual process leading to our final goal, whereby we can participate in the divine nature (cf. 2 P 1:4), not in the divine essence but through the uncreated energies of God's love.[6]

This is never pantheism. Eastern Christianity, as we have pointed out earlier, carefully distinguishes between the incomprehensible nature or essence of God which we human beings cannot grasp, and the uncreated energies of God's love. The divine energies are not things, but the inter-personal relations of the divine Father, Son and Holy Spirt in the order of salvation as each works in the oneness of God's nature as love to give himself to us at all times as uncreated grace.

Theosis or divinization is the result of the hypostatic union of the two natures of Christ. It results from the power of Christ's incarnation and resurrection, and from the outpouring of the

Holy Spirit. Our human nature has been restored by God through the incarnation and now is capable of participating in the divine nature of the Holy Trinity by the grace of the Holy Spirit. Thus everything that is holy and divinized is so, not by its own power or nature, but ony by participation in the Spirit's gift of *theosis* or divinization. This, however, requires the free and conscious cooperation on our part with the Holy Spirit. The work of the Spirit is inseparable from the work of the Son and the Heavenly Father.

Thus every Christian, anointed by the Holy Spirit, is able to enter into an intimate spousal relationship with Christ, thanks to the community of the Church and the role of the Paraclete, without fear of an "absorption" or of disappearing as a person. The Spirit in his role as the substantial love of the Trinity "disappears" or conceals himself by working in the individual Christian in order to aid him/her to reach perfect unity with Christ and through Christ with the Father.

In Christ we become through the Holy Spirit receptacles of the trinitarian act of God. Unity with God is achieved through love and divinization, and these are the works of the Holy Spirit. *Theosis* in its full realization belongs to the *eschaton*, namely, to the future life in the world to come. Then, our resurrection and the divinization of all things in Christ will be the fulfilling work of the "life-giving Spirit" (Jn 6:63).

If we are to reach any degree of divinization or participation in God's nature (2 P 1:4), we must cooperate with the Spirit. We must become loving, which is always personal, dynamic and self-emptying. Jesus said that the person who "is born of the Spirit is spirit" (Jn 3:6). The Holy Spirit, as the Eastern Fathers have always insisted upon after St. Athanasius, is the image of Jesus Christ. And we are to become the image of the Holy Spirit.

In a word, therefore, divinization is the realization of the likeness to the Son of God in the Holy Spirit. It is becoming love as God is love.

A CONTINUED PROCESS OF CONVERSION

THE Spirit works on every level of our human nature, including the unconscious levels of our psyche; yet he always works in gentleness and respect for our human free will. By giving us a healthy disgust with our state of tepidity, the Spirit makes a continued conversion possible, provided we accept his aid to destroy in us our sins and their effects.

More positively the Spirit moves us to a more complete love toward God and neighbor by bringing us into a more intimate, loving relationship with Christ who communicates to us a share in the triune divine life. Both the negative and positive aspects of a true conversion (namely, the uprooting of the passions and habits of selfishness and the putting on the mind of Christ) intermesh, rather than one following the other. As we cease living outside of God's love by our sinfulness, we will become children of God. But also, through the power of the Spirit, we will become more aware of our deeper areas of brokenness and "not yet" condition.

The true *metanoia* of the Spirit, therefore, is a continued call to conversion away from our bias toward self to greater regeneration into a divinized son/daughter of God. Such a state of tension between the "already" and the "not yet" never has a termination.

THE GIFTS OF THE HOLY SPIRIT

BESIDES the created sanctifying grace that becomes effective in our lives when we cooperate freely with his call, the Spirit operates also through his special gifts, fruits and virtues (theological and moral) to make us holy and righteous. We should keep in mind that the saints and mystics never make any distinction in their own experience between the grace of the virtues and that of the gifts of the Spirit. Even a complicated system like that developed by Thomas Aquinas, serves to highlight the inter-relation between the pure supernatural gifts of the Spirit and our own frail, but free cooperation with the Spirit.[7]

The Spirit of love invades all our faculties and covers all our actions, so that as we cooperate with his grace we can develop all the virtues needed to live an integrated and holy life unto the glory of God. If we keep this in mind, we will not be inclined to separate the natural and supernatural spheres. The Spirit's uncreated energies of love call us to cooperate in the inter-personal relations of the indwelling Trinity that truly effect our sanctification. Yet all is still grace from God's Spirit of love.

Love of God permeates all the details of our human life and conduct. The Spirit is the fundamental gift in his person as he adapts himself to our situations and circumstances. The Spirit develops love in us through many forms and manifestations. As Yves Congar points out,[8] the scriptural source of the theology of the gifts of the Spirit is the messianic text of Is 11:1-2:

> . . . on him the spirit of Yahweh rests,
> a spirit of wisdom and insight,
> a spirit of counsel and power,
> a spirit of knowledge and of the fear of Yahweh. . . .

The Septuagint and Vulgate texts have added to fear the gift of piety, thus giving us the seven traditional gifts of the Spirit.

Thomas Aquinas saw the necessity to highlight our own fragile power to choose always to act virtuously as befitting the call to be a divinized child of God. Hence these seven traditional gifts (wisdom, understanding, counsel, fortitude, knowledge, fear and piety) stand for the working of the Spirit immediately and directly to produce the work of sanctification. The Spirit uses us to cooperate through the virtues that are permeated by his grace, but the gifts are the operations of the Spirit operating freely, immediately, directly upon us. When our virtues are no longer sufficient for the accomplishment of the process of divinization, the Spirit intervenes and carries on the work by using his seven gifts.[9]

VIRTUES AND FRUITS OF THE SPIRIT

THE moral virtues of prudence, temperance, fortitude and justice are preparatory to our union with God. Yet for entering into the divinizing unity of love with the indwelling Trinity, we need the Spirit's infusion of the theological virtues of faith, hope and love. Yet even the virtues are in need of the seven gifts to be exercised to obtain the goal for which the Spirit infuses them into us.

Thomas Aquinas gives us an example of this. The action of the Spirit perfects the virtue of faith through the gift of infused understanding, and brings it to an inner penetration beyond anything we could obtain by way of cooperation with the Spirit.[10] Thus virtues are managed by us, and without the gifts the work of sanctification or divinization is impossible.

Thomas describes the fruits of the Holy Spirit as the ultimate and delightful products of the action of the Spirit in us.[11] We could say with Lucien Cerfaux, the Pauline scholar, that they are the "harvest of the Spirit.[12] Paul uses the singular for fruit, implying the gathering of the harvest of the working of the Spirit in our lives with our own cooperation to bring forth the culmination of the Spirit's operation in us. "What the Spirit brings is very different: love, joy, peace, patience, kindness, goodness, trustfulness, gentleness and self-control" (Gal 5:22).

Commentators suggest that this Pauline list[13] is an ideal portrait of the Christian living in the unique gift of the Spirit of love and surrendering to the operations of the Spirit in great peace and joy, "ready to welcome and calmly and patiently open to love his fellow-man."[14]

THE SPIRIT PRAYS IN US

THERE is an intimate relationship between one's level of intimacy attained in prayer when one is alone with God, and one's relationships with other human beings and the entire world. As we pray, so we live. As in prayer we exercise through the gifts of the Holy Spirit dwelling within us and operating in faith, hope and love, so we become transformed into our true uniqueness in Christ. Where our treasure is, there also is our heart, the center of our value system (Mk 12:34).

Yet as Paul writes, we for many reasons do not know how to pray as we ought:

> The Spirit too comes to help us in our weakness. For when we cannot choose words in order to pray properly, the Spirit himself expresses our plea in a way that could never be put into words, and God who knows everything in our hearts knows perfectly well what he means, and that the pleas of the saints expressed by the Spirit are according to the mind of God (Rm 8:26-27).

The Holy Spirit, who dwells within us, is the surrendering love within the community of the Trinity. Such love penetrates "the depths of everything, even the depths of God" (1 Cor 2:11). The depths of our very being, of our heart, can only be known by the Holy Spirit. In our prayer, he moves us beyond what our carnal mindedness might see as important, and instead leads us to ask for what God wants us to have.

The power of the Spirit's deeper faith, hope and love raises our consciousness to the primal experience of being known and loved personally by the Father and Son through the Spirit. In such a state, we find ourselves constantly being divinized and renewed in the depths of our being. We begin to experience what Paul writes: "Your mind must be renewed by a spiritual revolution so that you can put on the new self that has been created in God's way, in the goodness and holiness of the truth" (Eph 4:23-24).

The Spirit himself desires within us beyond any desires we could articulate. He puts the spark of such a desire of greater love of God and neighbor into our hearts, that can flame out in the burning fire of active love in our daily living. The Spirit allows us to cry out in our spirit "Abba" and know we are already heirs of God and co-heirs with Christ forever (Rm 8:15-16; Gal 4:6).

GROWTH IN AWARENESS OF GOD

THE work of the Spirit in developing our prayer life leads us to an ever-growing awareness that God and we form a union in love. Christian prayer in the Spirit of Jesus is an ongoing process of discovering not only the abyss that separates the all-holy God from us sinners, but also the depth of union that already exists between us and God.

Growth in prayer is, therefore, a growth in awareness of

God through the enlightenment of the Spirit, especially as he lives and acts through his infinite love within us. Our response in self-surrendering love pushes our consciousness of our new identity with God to new heights. Each time we encounter God in a prayerful experience, because of the working of the Spirit, we seem to enter into a fresh, new oneness in love with the Trinity.

CONTEMPLATIVE PRAYER

MOST of us are moved through the illumination of the Holy Spirit into formal prayer through a method of "meditation." We start with the great mysteries of Scripture to meet the living Word that has come down from the Father to teach us about him. We start with a passage from the Old or New Testaments, reading it slowly, pausing to reflect with our discursive powers of imagination, understanding and will.

As we cooperate in such disciplined prayer, the Spirit moves us more and more deeply into the presence of the risen Lord Jesus. As we learn to open up to the alluring power of the Spirit calling us to go deeper into ourselves, there is a new listening to God's presence, both within us and around us, throughout the busy day, in all his working in our lives.

The Spirit dries up the usual consoling feelings we may have had, and darkens our clear and distinct ideas of God. A dull sense of alienation comes over us as we seem to enter more deeply within ourselves. Faith is deepening without the props of sensible consolation, images and words. The more we advance into this darkness, the more names about God and his attributes have no meaning.

The Spirit creates this necessary pruning in order that greater union with the indwelling Trinity can be possible. It is a crying out for God to show himself in the night of the inner desert, where Christians can understand their own absolute nothingness before the *allness* of God. They begin to cry out in deep, dark, stark faith for the mercy of God: "Lord, Jesus Christ, have mercy on me."

An increase in hope and love through the infusion of the Spirit is evident as one begins to see that prayer now is a state of being toward the Trinity in praise and worship. Such a Christian lives in God's holy presence and surrenders in each event to his uncreated, loving energies. The Spirit makes it possible for the person of contemplative prayer to "be happy at all times; pray constantly and for all things give thanks to God, because this is what God expects you to do in Christ Jesus" (1 Th 5:17-18).

CALLED TO FREEDOM

IN the Gospels, Jesus speaks at length about God's love and our need to be transformed by that love through his outpouring Spirit in order to be a freeing love toward all other human beings. Jesus' whole work during his earthly life and now through his resurrectional presence living in us and in the Church, especially through the sacraments, was to release within us his Spirit who would bring about this freeing love in our lives.

Jesus preached about the Kingdom of God breaking in upon those who heard him, and he is now effecting by his abiding presence as risen Lord through his indwelling Spirit. He has been sent by the Father "to proclaim liberty to captives" (Lk 4:18; Is 61:1-2). The Spirit leads us into the whole truth of the gospel (Jn 16:13). He convinces us that Jesus is "the Way, the Truth and the Life" (Jn 14:6). He allows us to remain as branches fed by Christ the vine (Jn 15:1) in order to bring forth great fruit of love toward others.

Thus we cannot experience God's freeing love except through the Holy Spirit (Gal 5:16). Where the Spirit is, there is freedom (2 Cor 3:17). The Spirit frees us from slavery "to enjoy the same freedom and glory as the children of God" (Rm 8:21).

Christianity is not a law, although it contains one. It is not a morality, although it also possesses one. Paul points out to us: "But now we are rid of the Law, freed by death from our imprisonment, free to serve in the new spiritual way and not the old way of a written law" (Rm 7:6-7). The Old Law was powerless to transform us until the Word became flesh and gave us his indwelling Spirit.

The Spirit of Jesus brings us Christian freedom. This goes beyond mere external observance of the law. It means positively to be guided by the Spirit from within. "If you are led by the Spirit, no law can touch you" (Gal 5:19). Perfect freedom for the Christian consists in being guided at all times by the Holy Spirit who dwells within. The Spirit has swallowed up all laws; as love, he is the only criterion to guide us in all our thoughts, words and actions. We observe all laws when we live in the Spirit's love.

But such freeing love of the Spirit always drives us outward to live in loving service. We will discuss in the following chapter how the Spirit builds the Body of Christ, the Church, and how we reconcile obeying an external authority in the Church with our obeying only the Spirit of love. It is within the Church that we can discern the true Spirit of Jesus operating in her written and oral traditions.

True freedom, therefore, consists in our freely taking our entire life and giving it back to God, the Giver of all life, in adoration and worship, as total oblation. It is to allow the Spirit of love to guide us at every moment. The greatest aim in our earthly life is to surrender freely to the Holy Spirit, to the pursuing, passionate love of God toward us.

To conclude this chapter on the working of the Holy Spirit, I would like to quote the dramatic words of a modern martyr, the Jesuit Father Alfred Delp, hanged by the Nazis on Feb. 2, 1945. With his chained hands he wrote these words because interiorly he was truly free:

> The Holy Spirit is the passion with which God loves himself. Man has to correspond to that passion. He has to ratify it, and accomplish it. If he learns how to do this, the world will once again become capable of true love. We cannot know and love God unless God himself seizes hold of us and tears us away from our selfishness. God has to love himself in and through us and we shall then live in God's truth and love will once more become the living heart of the world.[15]

CHAPTER NINE

The Holy Spirit Fashions The Body Of Christ

THE SPIRIT BROODS OVER THE UNIVERSE

TODAY we are seeing revolutionary changes around our world in the political, economic, ecological, military and religious arenas. The Holy Spirit of the risen Lord is working powerfully in the hearts of millions of people, leading them to strive for greater freedom to live a fully human life in dignity, befitting God's human children.[1]

The whole world is charged with God's energizing power and love. God freely creates the world as a gift of love to us. We stand in the created world as God's masterpiece, to whom he entrusts its richness, "to cultivate and take care of it" (Gn 2:15). We are created and endowed with body, soul and spirit relationships to God and the rest of the created world. God invites us to receive his gifts of love and to decide freely to return that love by giving ourselves to God and neighbor. This invitation and our decision are the work of the Spirit. Still, we have the horrendous power, as history so often shows, to refuse God's Spirit of love.

To be human means, therefore, to become ever more free in each choice made out of love as we respond to God's call to be free in his Spirit. Our human dignity consists in affirming our true selfhood through self-emptying, loving service to others. God calls us unto communion with his own divine life, but on terms of our human freedom and responsiveness to the movements of his Spirit of love penetrating all of creation. God never coerces us, but through his Spirit he gently persuades us by "alluring" acts of divine, suffering love.

A COMMUNITY OF LOVING SERVICE

THE Holy Spirit urges us outward, to labor incessantly to bring Jesus forth in all human beings, made by God according to his image and likeness (Gn 1:26-27), that is Christ. We discover with Paul that the Spirit is the builder of the Christian community:

> Bear with one another charitably, in complete selflessness, gentleness and patience. Do all you can to preserve the unity of the Spirit by the peace that binds you together. There is one Body, one Spirit, just as you were all called into one and the same hope when you were called. There is one Lord, one faith, one baptism, and one God who is Father of all, through all and within all (Eph 4:2-6).

God's love is not solely toward the individual. It is universal and embraces all mankind. Hence the test of the Spirit's true working within our life is found in our love and humble service toward the neighbor. This is also the degree of our belonging to the Church, the Body of Christ.

Jesus sends us his Spirit that we may become members of his Body, the Church, and minister in love and humble service toward others. This was the life of Jesus on earth, and it is the sign that we are his disciples and that he lives within us and among us. The risen Jesus is found now in his Church. He is the vine, we are his branches, called to bring forth by the Spirit abundant fruit: to love one another as he loves us (Jn 13:16-17).

We are healthy members of the Church when we allow the Spirit of the risen Jesus to transform us inwardly so that we can, at all times, love and serve each other and the rest of mankind so that Jesus will be all in all. God is calling all human persons to become living and active love through the Spirit working in them. In the words of P.C. Mozoomdar:

> All men see the Spirit, most men ignore him, exceedingly few realize him. . . . That amid the chances, changes, and delusions of life, this one reality may cast his unfailing radiance in all dark places, and make myriad manifestations of himself that we may hold by him, dwell in him, know, love, and trust him at all times with the certainty and security we long for, faithful men in every age have spoken to us their experiences. These experiences are so simple and natural that under certain conditions of mental awakening they exact universal response. . . . Whatever ultimate mysteries there may be in the great depths of the Eternal Being, there is no expression that makes such a direct appeal to the restless instincts of our nature as that God is, that he is near, that he is in the heart, and that he is great and good, and we had better fly to him as to our refuge and home.[2]

THE CHURCH IS BORN

WHEN on Pentecost the apostles received the outpouring of the Holy Spirit promised by Jesus, they changed radically.

Externally they were truly "clothed with the power from on high" as they preached mightily, as they saw the sick healed by their touches, as they filled others with the Holy Spirit by their prayer and by imposing their hands upon them.

But the deepest change was an interior one. They were consciously aware at all times that the Spirit of Jesus was within them, guiding them. The greatest revelation was to experience a new sense of brotherhood, one with each other. They had first glimpsed such a oneness at the last supper when Jesus had given them his body and blood as their food and drink. It was there in that first Eucharist that the apostles felt the unity of the embryonic Body of Christ taking form for the first time. The Holy Spirit was begetting the New Creation: the risen Lord Jesus as the Head, one organically with the individual members of his Body, the Church.

John records Jesus' prayer for his followers that they would continue in that oneness, so intimate that he compared it to his union with the Father:

> Father, may they be one in us,
> as you are in me and I am in you,
> so that the world may believe it was you who sent me.
> I have given them the glory you gave to me,
> that they may be one as we are one.
> With me in them and you in me,
> may they be so completely one
> that the world will realize that it was you who sent me
> and that I have loved them as much as you loved me
> (Jn 17:21-23).

Jesus compared this oneness between himself and his followers to that found in the vine with its branches. The life-giving power flows from Jesus the vine through all the member-branches. As long as they abide in him, they will bring forth great fruit. But without Jesus they were like dry sticks of dead wood (Jn 15:1 ff.).

Christ died and went away, i.e., he gave up his earthly way of being present to his followers, only to acquire a new presence. "I will not leave you orphans; I will come back to you" (Jn 14:18). "I am going away, but shall return" (Jn 14:28). By sending his Spirit into the hearts of his disciples, Jesus makes them aware that he is now living within each member. The role of the Spirit in creating the Church can never diminish the fact that Jesus risen is the Head and extends his presence in time and space to bring salvation to contemporary society. The Spirit makes it possible that we can become living members of Christ and thus fulfill the mutual missions both of the Son and the Father.

IMAGES OF THE CHURCH

THE Spirit fashions the Church according to the image and likeness of Jesus Christ, who possesses both a divine and a human nature. Through the Spirit the Body also takes on a sharing in the dual natures of Christ. We remain through the Spirit uniquely and forever human, but divinized into the likeness and oneness with Jesus Christ.

Dr. Petro B.T. Bilaniuk[3] presents us with a list of some of the many expressions the early Church used to describe itself as the Spirit's new creation: the Body of Christ, the Kingdom of Heaven, the Kingdom of God, Disciples, Galileans, the Poor, the Christians, the Faithful, the Saints, the Brothers, the true Israel, the Israel of God, the Israel according to the Spirit, the Seed of Abraham, the Circumcision, the People of God, the Household of God, the Temple of God, the Adorers of God, the Catholics, the Fishes, the Alive, the Strangers, the Pilgrims, etc.

In more modern times we find such titles as the Bride of Christ, the Living Christ, the Mystical Christ, the Mystical Body of Christ, the Church of the Holy Spirit, etc. One image, that of the Church as the Family of God, has surely been eclipsed in Western Christianity. In Eastern Christianity, as the Russian Bishop Cassian Besobrasove points out,[4] the sublime mystery of the Trinity as a community of interpersonal relationships is experienced as sharing their family unity in uniqueness with those who live in Christ through his Spirit.

Paul states that Jesus is "the ruler of everything, the head of the Church, which is his body, the fullness of him who fills the whole creation" (Eph 1:23). He continues:

> But now in Christ Jesus, you that used to be so far apart from us have been brought very close, by the blood of Christ. For he is the peace between us, and has made the two into one and broken down the barrier which used to keep them apart, actually destroying in his own person the hostility caused by the rules and decrees of the Law. This was to create one single New Man in himself out of the two of them and by restoring peace through the cross, to unite them both in a single Body and reconcile them with God. In his own person he killed the hostility. Later he came to bring the good news of peace, peace to you who were far away and peace to those who were near at hand. Through him, both of us have in the one Spirit our way to the Father (Eph 2:13-18).

The New Man is the archetype of the human race, those of humanity who have died to the old creation and live now in Christ as a "new creation" (2 Cor 5:17). This New Adam, the total Christ, has been created in "the goodness and holiness of the truth" (Eph 4:24). He is unique because in him the boundaries between any one group and the rest of the human race all disappear:

> You have stripped off your old behavior with your old self, and you have put on a new self which will progress toward true knowledge the more it is renewed in the image of its creator; and in that image there is no room for distinction between Greek and Jew, between the circumcised or the uncircumcised, or between the barbarian and Scythian, slave and free man. There is only Christ: he is everything and he is in everything (Col 3:9-11).

F.X. Durrwell insists that Paul means that a new man has come into a new form of existence. It is not that Jesus exerts simply an influence upon the Christian, but the latter enters through the working of the Holy Spirit into an ontological relation of oneness with Jesus, "by a change transforming him into 'one man, one body' (Eph 2:15-16) — into the bodily Christ."[5]

THE BODY OF CHRIST — THE CHURCH

PAUL uses the Greek word, *ekklesia* (which literally translates the Hebrew, *Qahal*, or the called out People of God, the Chosen Ones) to refer to the Church about sixty times with a variety of meanings. As his ecclesiology developed along with his understanding of Christ's relationships to his members, so he gives different meanings to the concept of the Church.

Whether he uses it to refer to a specific assembly of Christian believers, e.g., in the churches of Asia (1 Cor 16:19) or to the universal Church (1 Cor 12:18), Paul sees it as a community, a *koinonia* or familial fellowship, of Christian believers linked together by the bonds of faith and sacraments. The sacraments are especially Baptism which incorporates the members into the community, and the Eucharist which symbolizes the union of the members with the physical Body of Christ and deepens that union. There is also the bond of obedience to the bishops and presbyters empowered by Christ to teach his word with his own authority.

A definite progression is seen in Paul's understanding of Christ's relationship with his members. Earlier, Paul stressed the living Christ as the source of the common, supernatural life within the believing Christian. He then moved to a greater understanding of the Church as identified in some manner with the physical, resurrected Body of Jesus Christ. In his major epistles the concept of the identity of the Body and Christ the Head is not fully developed, e.g., where he clearly distinguishes that we are together "Christ's body, but each of you is a different part of it" (1 Cor 12:27).

In his later epistles, especially in Colossians and Ephesians, he clearly identifies the Christian people as the Body of Christ, one with him. Christ loves this Body, the Church, cherishing and nourishing it. ". . . it is this body and we are its living parts" (Eph 5:30). Christ is the Head who nourishes and strengthens the whole Body with a divine growth (Col 2:19). The whole Body is dependent on Christ. Each part is harmoniously knitted together and transformed through the Spirit who comes from Jesus Christ. The Body grows and builds itself up through love (Eph 4:6; Col 1:19, 24; Eph 1:22, 23; 4:15; 5:23).

The Church is intimately related to the risen Christ, who is "the ruler of everything, the head of the Church, which is his Body. . . ." (Eph 1:20-23).[6]

THE MYSTICAL BODY

AS the Holy Spirit overshadowed Mary and the Word became flesh through the Spirit, so the Spirit begets the oneness of Christians with Christ in the Church as the Mystical Body of Christ. Unfortunately the word *mystical* in the West has lost its original Greek sense. For many of us it connotes something rather nebulous and unearthly. It seems to imply that Christ is present to the members of his Body-Church by either a moral or some "ethereal" union. In contrast, Paul teaches an ontological *real* presence of the risen Jesus who through his Spirit shares his very own glorious life with his members.

Pierre Benoit, O.P. describes this union as a physical reality of a unique type. The spiritual (*pneumatic*) body of the living, risen Christ (1 Cor 15:44) is the bestower of the regenerated life of salvation to human beings. It is under the form of a physical (sacramental) union of the body of the Christian with the individual risen body of Christ. "Without a doubt this 'physical' reality is of a very special type, completely new which is that of the eschatological era begun while the old era still continues."[7]

The risen Savior lives within the individual Christian, releasing his Holy Spirit that the members may go out to the other actual or potential members of Christ's Body and by love let the Spirit bind them into a greater union. The term *Mystical Body* is a legitimate theological development out of St. Paul's teaching. It presents to us an orthodox doctrine that avoids on the one hand a purely physical union with Christ and, on the other, a purely moral aggregate.

Christ, therefore, in his risen, glorified life through his spiritualized "physical" body lives through grace in the members of his body, the Church. This relationship between Christ and his members admits an ongoing growth process that will continue even into life after death.

ALWAYS THE SAME SPIRIT

JESUS is present to his members through the Holy Spirit. "Each one of us, however, has been given his own share of grace, given as Christ allotted it" (Eph 4:7). It is truly Jesus living in each member in a unique way, quite different from the way he lives and operates in someone else. Jesus lives in us through the charisms that his Spirit effects for the good of the whole. Our talents become charisms when we cover them with the Spirit's graces and use them to build up the Body of Christ, the Church:

> There is a variety of gifts but always the same Spirit; there are all sorts of service to be done, but always to the same Lord; Working in all sorts of different ways in different people, it is the same God who is working in all of them. The particular way in which the Spirit is given to each person is for a good purpose. . . . All these are the work of one and the same Spirit, who distributes different gifts to different people just as he chooses (1 Cor 12:4-12).

Paul inserts within this quote the nine gifts of the Spirit given to build up the Church at Corinth. This was not meant to be an exclusive listing. These charisms are: wisdom, knowledge, faith, healing, miracles, prophecy, discernment, speaking in tongues and interpretations of the tongues.

THE CHARISM OF AUTHORITY

PAUL also gives us various other lists of charisms. One important list concerns the gifts that build up the Body of Christ through the hierarchy, given by Christ to his Church to maintain harmony and order: "And to some, his gift was that they should be apostles; to some, prophets; to some, evangelists; to some, pastors and teachers; so that the saints together make a unity in the work of service, building up the body of Christ. . . ." (Eph 4:11-13).

A special presence of the working of the Spirit in the Body of Jesus is that of *authority*. Individual freedom in the Spirit cannot contradict the same voice of the Spirit in the external authority Christ has given to the Church, also to build it up.

The Church is holy and yet it is made up of sinful men and women. It is partially divine by God's gifts of the sacraments and the preached Word. Yet it is human and very material. It is to have no part of the world's thinking, yet it is necessarily in the world as a leaven. As the Bride of Christ, the Church shares in his power and holiness through the Spirit. Yet the Church also is the prostitute needing conversion and reform. It shares in Christ's shepherding of the lost, but it is also the lost sheep that always needs to be found by God.

We need to see the loving presence of Jesus and his Spirit, the "two hands of the Father," working in the duly appointed authority in a divine-human Church on the horizontal plane. Perhaps nowhere else is the tension between light and darkness seen better than in the area of Christ's authority exercised by human instruments. They can so easily fail to be "charismatic" and completely open to and guided by the Holy Spirit to use their gifts as the suffering servant, Jesus, served his followers. Yves Congar on this point well writes:

> In a society such as ours, which is individualistic to the point of anarchy, we must, without losing sight of the extremely profound theme of Christian freedom, remember the Christian idea of obedience. Obedience is not just a matter of what we have to do for one another, through one another, in view of our common destiny according to the plan of God; obedience effects an important segment of the truth of inter-membral

relationships within a differentiated and ordered body (God is not a God of disorder. . . . 1 Cor 14:33). While effecting the interlocking of the members in this body, it also effects an acknowledgment of the lordship of Christ, master of order. . . . Every christian encounters Christ in his brothers and in his superiors (even the difficult ones! 1 P 2:18) or subordinates, and he is called to realize his life as a life "in the Lord," in this very situation, in these very encounters.[8]

THE SACRAMENTS

THE essential work of the dual, but not separable, missions of Jesus and the Spirit is to fashion the "called out People of God" into the Church that is one, holy, catholic and apostolic.[9] "There is one body, one Spirit, just as you were all called into one and the same hope when you were called. There is one Lord, one faith, one baptism, and one God who is Father of all, over all, through all and within all" (Eph 4:4-6).

The Spirit brings about a oneness in faith, in sacraments (especially through Baptism and the Eucharist) and in harmony through loving obedience to the teaching magisterium in the Church.

Let us see the work of the Spirit in making us into a one, holy, catholic and apostolic Body of Christ through the sacraments. The sacraments are sacred signs made up of words and actions, employing material symbols in which Jesus Christ through his Spirit bestows upon us an increase of his divine life. We celebrate our new divine life in him; but also he communicates that divine life to us as we in faith, hope and love open ourselves to him through the infusion of the Holy Spirit in such a liturgical encounter.

Baptism through the calling down (*epiklesis*) of the Holy Spirit brings us into unity in the Body of Christ, the Church.

We become living members as we receive the forgiveness of all previous sins and also a new life of grace by being born from above by the Spirit (Jn 3:1-6). In one Spirit we are baptized into one Body, that of the total Jesus Christ (1 Cor 12:13). He is our Head, we his members.

Confirmation gives us the full power of a matured Christian. As adults we receive a fuller release of the Spirit to make us witnesses of our faith to the world.

In the Eucharist we receive Jesus as he prolongs his death and resurrection in us. We receive his life that enables us to share in his death and resurrection. A prominent place is given in the Eucharistic Liturgy to the *epiklesis*[10] or the calling down of the Holy Spirit upon the gifts of bread and wine to transform them into the body and Blood of Christ. In the Eastern Christian Churches such a calling down of the Spirit is highlighted in all the sacraments, testifying to St. Basil's statement: "Creatures do not have any gift on their own; all good comes from the Holy Spirit."[11]

In Reconciliation we are not only forgiven our sins, but Jesus touches us in a deep healing of the "roots" of our sinfulness.

In Marriage a baptized man and woman are joined by Jesus Christ in the Spirit, bestowing the grace of a lifelong union. This gives them grace to love each other and the children coming from that marriage as Jesus loves and gives himself to his Church (Eph 5:28-29).

In Orders, Jesus Christ shares his priesthood of the New Covenant with certain "called" people. The bishop has the fullness of this sacrament and can ordain priests and consecrate bishops, and is the ordinary minister of Confirmation. Priests assist the bishop, celebrate the other sacraments, preach and build up the Body of Christ.

The Anointing of the Sick aids us both to a healing on the body, soul and spirit levels, and above all to a happy death. St.

James describes this sacrament as the anointing with oil to heal the body and to forgive sins (Jn 5:13-16).

Thus not only the sacraments of initiation (Baptism, Confirmation and the Eucharist) but every sacrament of the Church has pneumatological and divinizing meaning.

THE HOLY SPIRIT SENDS US FORTH

YOU and I touch God the Father in Jesus Christ, his Son, through the Spirit in God's Word and in the sacraments within the Christian community, the Body of Christ. We Christians are drawn outward by the Spirit into the world around us to bring about a union of love as we cooperate to build the Body of Christ. It is the work of the Spirit of love who moves us outward in loving service toward others.

St. Dorotheus of the 6th century used the example of a wheel. The closer the spokes of the wheel move to the center, the closer they come to each other. The farther they move out from the center, the more distance separates one spoke from one another. Our faith in God's love for us and our return of that love to God by words alone are dead unless we manifest unselfish love to others in need. "If one of the brothers or one of the sisters is in need of clothes and has not enough food to live on, and one of you says to them, 'I wish you well, keep yourself warm and eat plenty,' without giving them the bare necessities of life, then what good is that? Faith is like that; if good works do not go with it, it is quite dead" (Jm 2:13-17).

A RECONCILER

AS we grow in the love of God, the Spirit moves us to go out in self-sacrificing love toward others. We become concerned with any and all their needs, be they material, psychic or spiritual. We wish to share with others the love, joy and peace that we abundantly and habitually receive from God in prayer and in the sacraments.

We become more aware daily that we are called to be instruments of peace, reconcilers of people living in disharmony with themselves, with God and with the world around them. "All things are of God who has reconciled us to himself by Jesus Christ and has given to us the ministry of reconciliation" (2 Cor 5:18).

Now there are no strangers for us, but only sisters and brothers of one Father through Jesus Christ and his Spirit. And when we anguish as to what more we can do for others in need, we find the call to humbly pray that they all may be one as Christ and the Father are one (cf. Jn 17:22-23).

THE COSMIC CHRIST

EVEN outside of the official Church, Christ gives himself to all human beings of whatever nationality, culture or religion. Vatican Council II repeatedly chose to describe the Church as the "universal sacrament of salvation."[12] Today theologians search for new ways of expressing how the Spirit reveals Christ's presence and activity both inside and outside the ecclesial, sacramental system.

Contact with non-Western cultures and non-Christian religions has expanded our perspectives of the working presence of Christ in our world. Wider contacts with other philosophical, theological and cultural expressions can refine and enrich the timeless elements in Christianity.

Our very secular pursuits, though not sacral as such, must not contradict but complement the activities of Christ as his Spirit with our cooperation builds up his Body in his established Church-Community. Edward Schillebeeckx sums up the relationship between the two distinct but complementary orders:

> This means that in the plan of salvation the concrete world, by definition, is an implicit Christianity; it is an objective, non-sacral but saintly and sanctified expression of mankind's communion with the living God, whereas the Church *qua* institution of salvation, with her explicit creed, her worship and sacraments, is the direct and sacral expression of that identical communion — she is the *separata a mundo* (un-worldly). To speak of the relationships between the Church and the world does not mean therefore that a dialogue is to be launched between the religious and the profane, between the supernatural and the natural or intraworldly — it is rather a dialogue between two complementary authentically Christian expressions of one and the same God-related life concealed in the mystery of Christ, namely, the ecclesial expression (in the strict sense of the word) and the worldly expression of that identically same life, internalized within human life through man's free acceptance of grace.
>
> In other words, the implicitly Christian and the explicitly Christian dimension of the same God-related life, that is, of human life hidden in God's absolute and gratuitous presence.[13]

ESCHATOLOGICAL HOPE

THE divine plan of salvation tends always toward a completion of God's inter-related creation. All material beings are God's gifts to be used and developed by us thinking human beings so that eventually creation will reach its fullness in Christ. "From the beginning till now the entire creation, as we know, has been groaning in one great act of giving birth; and not only creation, but all of us who possess the first-fruits of the Spirit, we too groan inwardly as we wait for our bodies to be set free" (Rm 8:22-23).

It is the glorified Christ who associates himself as mediator in bringing the universe to its appointed completion. He brings everything under subjection to him so that he can bring it back to his heavenly Father "so that God may be all in all" (1 Cor 15:28). In Jesus Christ the Father has destined that the fullness of the whole universe should dwell. He is reconciling, recapitulating, leading back to his heavenly Father the created universe, but one fulfilled by being one with Christ (Col 1:15-20).

The Body of Christ is his Church (Eph 5:23-30). But the Body of Christ must grow until it reaches its fullness (*pleroma*). Vatican II declares that the Church, or in other words, the kingdom of Christ now present in mystery, grows visibly through the power of God in the world:

> While she transcends all limits of time and of race, the Church is destined to extend to all regions of the earth and so to enter into the history of mankind . . . that moved by the Holy Spirit she may never cease to renew herself, until through the cross she arrives at the light which knows no setting.[14]

THE SPIRIT WORKS INVISIBLY

CHRIST lives in his Church through the Holy Spirit, guiding the members and the hierarchy to persevere in knowing and "in doing the truth" (Jn 3:21). But the Holy Spirit is also actively building up the Church, the Body of Christ, among those persons who are formally members of Christ's Church.

A stone tossed into a placid lake produces ripples that spread out into continuous concentric circles, moving from the center until the circles touch the landed shore. The Church is the center from which grace goes out to touch all parts of the world. At this center, generating the outward movement, are the sacraments. Chief among the sacraments is the Eucharist, which gives us Jesus Christ as physically present and acting among us. The circles spread out, becoming larger until they almost merge, but even here the impact of Christ, the *Pantocrator*, the Lord of the Universe, continues to be felt.[15] The Holy Spirit moves each of us toward unity in Christ. The Church is increasing wherever one opens up to act in true love toward others. Karl Rahner well describes this invisible Christianity:

> Today we know that there exists an invisible Christianity where, under the effect of God's action, the justification of sanctifying grace is really found. Even though a man belonging to this hidden Christianity may deny it, claim that he does not know if he is a Christian or that he cannot state with certainty that Christ is the Son of God, he may all the same have been through grace the object of divine election.[16]

A NEW PENTECOST

WHEN Pope John XXIII announced on January 23, 1959, his plan to convoke the 21st Ecumenical Council of Vatican II, he prayed that the doors and windows of the Church would be opened and a fresh wind of the Spirit would blow through, sweeping away all that was deadening and letting the Holy Spirit renew through the Church the face of the earth.

Today, the Church is being given a new challenge to cooperate in the reconstruction of a more free and just world founded on the basic dignity of every human being.

The Church is not only the hierarchy of the ecclesiastical organization or even a nebulous spiritualized people who have been baptized. It embraces all who believe in Jesus Christ and who organize their lives to live with commitment according to the faith passed on through traditions and the sacraments. It builds itself up and therefore turns to the world in which such Christians live. It works to create a more just and harmonized world as they hear and speak the living Word of God and organize themselves around the hierarchy to carry out what they have heard and experienced.[17]

THE CHARISMATIC RENEWAL

THROUGHOUT the world, a gigantic outpouring of the Spirit's gifts upon groups and individuals is taking place. Such Christians are claiming their awareness of the indwelling Spirit. They are also attesting to the world around them in their daily lives that the Spirit is still opperating in his Church through his charisms or gifts exercised in love to build up the Body of Christ.

This general renewal has been manifested in biblical and liturgical renewal, in renewed efforts in preaching of the Word, in teaching catechetics, in the apostolate of the laity, in new forms of religious life and a spirituality of marriage, plus in the Catholic Church's social teachings and activities to preach and to put into effect a more just existence for all human beings.[18]

One specific form of charismatic renewal has taken on a most dramatic form, experienced by a great number of Christians of all walks of life around the world. This is the so-called "charismatic renewal" that first spread like fire among the Protestant Churches since 1956 and in the Catholic Church since 1967. Prayer groups prayed for the charismatic gifts of the Holy Spirit, and amazing Pentecosts happened again.

Vatican II's *Constitution on the Church* declares:

> Allotting his gifts "to everyone according as he will" (1 Cor 12:11), he [the Spirit] distributes special graces among the faithful of every rank. By these gifts he makes them fit and ready to undertake the various tasks of offices advantageous for the renewal and upbuilding of the Church. . . . [19]

As Heribert Mühlen, S.J., points out in regard to the rapid spread of this renewal among Catholics: "Who would have imagined that two years after the publication of this document (*Constitution on the Church*), some 1,500 prayer groups, attended regularly each week by about 200,000 Catholics including some bishops, would exist in the Catholic Church?"[20]

The Catholic charismatic renewal in the United States was highly influenced by the Pentecostal Churches that originated in 1901 in Topeka, Kansas and multiplied into the Holiness and the Assembly of God Churches. This renewal was described by some as the Catholic Pentecostal Movement, but it is not accepted as an adequate term. Now it usually is referred to as the Catholic Charismatic Renewal. In France, perhaps more fittingly, it is called the Renewal of the Spirit. To call it merely *charismatic* seemingly restricts the manifestations of some of the Spirit's charisms, especially by emphasizing those of 1 Cor 12, such as speaking and praying in tongues, prophecy and faith-healing.[21]

CRITIQUE OF THE CHARISMATIC RENEWAL

AT least in the Catholic charismatic movement there has been no serious rift away from the hierarchical teaching body. The sacraments are more frequented and there is evidence of a greater love for the study and praying out of Scripture. Most Catholic charismatics radiate joy and a faith to see God working in his providential care in all events of life.

There is, however, a great need for discernment of the working of the Holy Spirit. If "charismatic" means only those in such a renewal who pray in a certain manner, usually with great emotion and physical display of enthusiasm, then there is a grave danger of creating a "sect," a schism in the Body of Christ, hardly the work of the true Spirit.

A danger lies in attributing everything directly to the primary causality of God and ignoring science or any secondary cause. Some such "charismatics" who do this often ignore the findings of psychology and psychiatry as they are spurred on by powerful, emotional preachers and enthusiastic singing. The phenomenon of "falling" in the Spirit, for example, requires a proper discernment.

DISCERNMENT OF SPIRITS

AS Christians today seek to encounter God more immediately and directly through the release of the Holy Spirit, there develops a much greater need of discernment of spirits. One of the essential elements of our spiritual life is the ability to discern which movements of our "spirit" are from God's Spirit and which come from "ungodly" spirits. In the Old Testament there were true and false prophets. In the New Testament there were dissensions and various opposing teachers and practices.

The secret of a happy and successful Christian life that is

guided by the Spirit to build up the Body of Christ is to seek to do each thought, word and deed out of love for God. It is always to seek, as Jesus did in his earthly life, to please our heavenly Father in all things. We return God's love with deeds that are accomplished according to his holy will. But what does "doing the will" of God mean? This is what is meant by the gift of discernment of the Holy Spirit, given to those who are pure of heart.

First, we must believe that God has a will for us in our decisions and in every detail of our daily life. We must believe that his Spirit will be given to us so that we might discover what his will is. "Do not be thoughtless but recognize what is the will of the Lord . . . be filled with the Spirit" (Eph 5:17-18).

We must also desire to know God's will and be resolved to carry it out. We should strive to be of service to others in the community, as we seek to fulfill the commitments and duties of our state of live so as always to promote our return of love to God by never being self-seeking. [22]

SOME GUIDELINES

1. The first step in discernment is to be able sensitively to see differences in interior movements on the psychic and spiritual levels that take place in prayer. The disciplines of journaling and the evening examen are helps in developing such "feeling." [23]

2. Be cautious and discerning especially in judging the source of any religious or mystical experiences. Teachers of true Christian prayer have always insisted that visions, voices, levitation, odors and sweet tastes in the mouth, gentle touches by angelic messengers, etc. are never to be sought for in prayer. One must stress humility and compunction as the true touchstones of a

religious experience with no attention given to the physico-psychic effects. [24]

3. To discern whether the sense of peace and oneness with God we experience is really from the Holy Spirit, we must ask whether we are honestly seeking to surrender our lives to the dominance of the Spirit. The true index will be whether the Spirit's fruits of joy and peace send us out to serve others and bring us into a loving obedience to the teachings of the Church.

4. Following the discernment Jesus gives us: "You will know them by their fruits," (Mt 7:20), and that of St. Paul in the fruits of the Spirit (Gal 5:22), we can usually find the best index of the working of the Spirit in our lives. We must beware, however, of judging by only one or another fruit produced. How often seeming patience can be a cloak for apathy, affability for crowd acceptance, long-suffering for cowardliness! We must be aware of the principle in the spiritual life that the signs of the fruits of the Spirit usually appear as a unified growth. The growth is one of greater unity of personhood in self-giving love. It brings about a progressive increase in basic well-being, joy, peace, and consolation.

5. The help of a wise, prudent and holy director can be of great help in discerning the proper movements of the Holy Spirit.

PAROUSIA

CHRIST will come at the end of time to transform this universe by bringing it to its completion in and through his Spirit. Then Christ's work, which began after his death and resurrection and continued through his glorious risen life in mankind and in the whole sub-human cosmos, will be completed. In a real sense, the *parousia*, or final appearance of Christ in glory, is already present in our universe. He is now achieving the victory over cosmic evil, a victory that will be full and perfect only at the end of time.

In those in whom Christ is now living, he is overcoming the forces of death, sin and disorder. How the final transformation in the *parousia* will be brought about, God did not deem it necessary for us to know. Peter's dramatic description largely follows the Old Testament apocalyptic literature that used images favoring a total cataclysm: ". . . By that coming the heavens will be set afire and dissolved, and the elements will be burned up and melted" (1 P 3:10-13).

But for Paul, Christ is here and now forming his Body by his Spirit. This Body is, for Paul, a living entity of diverse members in whom Christ truly lives as the source of their new divine filiation. And his living members are to cooperate with him in reconciling the universe with God (2 Cor 5:17-19).

A TRANSFIGURED WORLD

CHRIST is actually, even now, absolute Head of the material created cosmos. But his primacy will not be completely recognized until his second coming when he will return in a mysterious way through his divinized members in his Body to lead the created world back to the Father.

The whole world will have reached its completion in being transfigured from its deformity, its "vanity" as Paul calls it, into a "renovated creation." Our world will not be annihilated, but transfigured. Through the incarnation and resurrection, and through his Spirit working in the members of his Body, Jesus brings about the process of recapitulating all things according to his Father's plan.

Jesus is the Alpha (Rv 1:17), the beginning, the image according to which we human beings and the entire material world have been created. He is for us also the Omega (Rv 1:17), the goal, the end toward which we are moving, drawn by the Holy Spirit. We become fully human only as incorporated in Christ Jesus. Those who deliberately stifle the Spirit of love in their lives and thus refuse to accept their fulfillment in Christ, eject themselves from the stream of humanity moving toward Christ. But the stream, as God intended and Scripture reveals to us flows on to its goal.

The whole created cosmos, including ourselves, is to be brought into the glorification of God. Jesus Christ in his Body through his Spirit is now accomplishing in the created universe the completion and fulfillment which his first coming began. His second coming in his living members will bring this to its earthly completion, so that God may be everything to everyone and everything (1 Cor 15:28).

CONCLUSION

WE now come to the end and also return to the beginning: the blessed and holy Trinity, the divine community of love. The work of the Spirit is to divinize us by his grace into sharers of the triune God's nature as love. "Love will come to its perfection in us when we can face the day of Judgment without fear; because even in this world we have become as he is" (1 Jn 4:17). "We shall be like him, because we shall see him as he really is" (1 Jn 3:2). We shall see and we shall be like the triune God.

According to Jesus (Jn 3:6) the person who is born of the Spirit is spirit. We are to become like the Holy Spirit who is self-emptying love. The Father divinizes us through the power of the Holy Spirit into the likeness of the Son. We will become love.

Allow me to conclude by quoting a hymn of divine love by St. Symeon the New Theologian (+ 1022):

> Being God, the Divine Spirit refashions completely those
>   whom he receives within himself.
> He makes them completely anew.
> He renews them in an amazing manner.
> How can he avoid taking on something of the same filth of
>   them?
> Not any more than fire takes on the black of iron;
>   but on the contrary it gives to it all of its own
>   properties.
> So likewise the Divine Spirit, incorruptible, gives
>   incorruptibility.
> Being immortal, he gives immortality.
> Because he is light that never sets,
>   he transforms all of them into light
>   in whom he comes down and dwells.
> And because he is life, he bestows life to all.
> As he is of the same nature as Christ, being of the same
>   essence as well as the same in glory,
>   and being united with him, he forms then absolutely
>   similar to Christ.
> For the Master is not jealous
>   that mortals should appear equal to himself by divine
>   grace, that he does not disclaim as unworthy,
>   his servants from becoming like to him.
> But rather he is happy and he rejoices
>   in seeing all of us, from mere human to become by
>   grace such as he was and is by nature.
> For he is our Benefactor
>   and he wishes that all of us become what he himself
>   is.

For if we are not strictly like unto him,
> how can we be united to him as he said?
How indeed can we remain in him
> if we are not such as he is?
How will he abide in us if we are not similar to him?
Therefore, as you wisely understand this,
>> hasten to receive the Spirit, who comes from God and
>> is divine,
>> in order that you may become such as my words have
>> explained,
>> heavenly and divine, such as the Master spoke of
>> in order to become heirs of the Heavenly Kingdom
>> forever. . . .
Run zealously, therefore, all of you, in order that you
>> may be
>> judged worthy to be found within the Kingdom of
>> Heaven and to reign
>> with Christ, the Master of all, to whom is due all glory
>> with the Father and the Spirit, for ages and ages.
>> Amen.[25]

End Notes

CHAPTER ONE

1. It is amazing that Christians have used the dove as a symbol for the Holy Spirit, for two thousand years without even knowing what it really means. "The precise significance of the dove had been the subject of much discussion. . . . There is no passage in the older literature in which the dove would be a clear and distinct symbol of the Holy Spirit." Joseph Fitzmyer, S.J.: *The Gospel according to Luke* (N.Y.: Doubleday, 1982), pp. 483-484.
2. Cf.: Yves M.J. Congar, O.P.: *I Believe in the Holy Spirit*: three volumes, tr. by David Smith (N.Y.: the Seabury Press, 1983), Vol 3, p. 4.
3. Congar, *op. cit.*, Vol. 1, pp. 37-38.
4. *Ibid.*, pp. 90, 92, note 16.
5. A.W. Wainright: *The Trinity in the New Testament* (London: SPCK, 1977), p. 199.
6. In: *Osservatore Romano*, English ed.. June 9, 1986, p. 1.
7. We might point out two excellent modern theological works on the Holy Spirit that move us toward a true understanding of his importance in our lives today. Cf.: Yves Congar, O.P., three volumes, *op. cit.*; and Luis M. Bermejo, S.J.: *The Spirit of Life: The Holy Spirit in the Life of the Christian* (Chicago: Loyola University Press, 1989).
8. St. Basil: *On the Holy Spirit* (Crestwood, N.Y.: St. Vladimir's Seminary Press, 1980), #47, p. 74.

9. Pseudo-Dionysius: *Mystical Theology*, in: *Dionysius the Areopagite. The Divine Names and the Mystical Theology*, tr. C.E. Rolt (London: SPCK, 1920), p. 19.

10. St. Irenaeus: *Against Heresies*, V, 6, in: *The Ante-Nicene Fathers*, I ed. by A. Roberts and J. Donaldson (Grand Rapids, MI: Eerdmans, 1962), pp. 531-532.

11. On a more detailed discussion of God's uncreated energies cf.: G. Maloney: *Uncreated Energy* (Warwick, N.Y.: Amity House, 1987).

12. *Ibid.*, pp. 59-80.

13. St. Bernard: *De Consideratione*, V, 11, 24, in: *PL* (Migne: *Patrologia Latina*), 182; 802B. Cf. also: *Serm. 88 de diversis*, I: *PL* 183; 706 and *In die Pent.*, *Serm.* 1, 1: *PL* 183; 323. Cited by Congar, *op. cit.*, Vol. 3, p. 9.

14. Pseudo-Dionysius: *On the Divine Names*, I, *op. cit.*, p. 70.

15. Congar, *op. cit.*, Vol. 3, p. 6.

16. Cyril of Jerusalem: *Cat. XVI*, 2, in: *PG* (Migne: *Patrologia Graeca*) 33; 920A.

17. St. Hilary of Poitiers: *The Trinity*, tr. by Stephen McKenna, C.SS.R., in: *The Fathers of the Church* (N.Y., 1954), Vol. 25, p. 36.

CHAPTER TWO

1. M.J. Scheeben: *The Mysteries of Christianity*, tr. by Cyril Vollert, S.J. (St. Louis: B. Herder Book Co., 1946), p. 45.

2. *Meister Eckhart*; ed. Franz Pfeiffer, 2 vols., tr. by C. de B. Evans (London: Watkins, 1947): *Sermon LVII, Divine Understanding*, p. 267.

3. Pseudo-Dionysius: *op. cit.*, p. 69.

4. Hilary of Poitiers: *The Trinity*, *op. cit.*, p. 41.

5. Gabriel Marcel: *Metaphysical Journal*, tr. by Bernard Wall (Chicago: Henry Regnery Co., 1952), pp. 62, 147, 221.

6. Raimundo Panikkar: *The Trinity and the Religious Experience of Man* (N.Y.: Orbis Books, 1973), p. 46.

CHAPTER THREE

1. Cf.: V. Lossky: *The Mystical Theology of the Eastern Church* (Cambridge & London: James Clarke & Co. Ltd., 1957), p. 71.
2. Karl Rahner: *The Trinity*, tr. by J. Donceel, S.J. (N.Y.: Herder & Herder, 1989), p. 22.
3. *Ibid.*, p. 101. Yves Congar agrees with the first half, that the Trinity is manifested in the economy of salvation, but he seeks to qualify the "vice-versa" that the "immanent Trinity is also the economic Trinity." Congar asks: "Can the free mystery of the economy and the necessary mystery of the Tri-unity of God be identified . . . even if God's creatures did not exist, God would still be a Trinity of Father, Son and Spirit, since creation is an act of free will, whereas the procession of the Persons takes place in the world itself, outside the immanent divine life. . . .," *op. cit.*, Vol. 3, p. 12.

   Piet Schoonenberg, S.J., in his work, *The Christ* (London & Sydney, 1972), develops in great detail in several theses an extension of Rahner's principle.
4. Roland Zimany: "Grace, Deification and Sanctification: East-West," in: *Diakonia*, Vol. 12 (1977), p. 125.
5. M.M. Scheeben: *op. cit.*, p. 445.
6. St. Augustine: *City of God*; XI, p. 26, in: *Fathers of the Church Series* tr. G. Walsh, S.J., and Sister Grace Monahan, O.S.V. (N.Y.: Fathers of the Church, 1952), p. 228.
7. Karl Rahner: *op. cit.*, p. 35.
8. H. Mühlen: *Der Heilige Geist als Person* (Munster: Aschendorff, 1966).
9. Richard of St. Victor: *De Trinitate*; Book III, c. 19: *PL* 196: 915B-930D.
10. Richard of St. Victor: *De Trinitate*, 3,2. ed. Jean Rabaillier, pp. 136-137.
11. *Ibid.*, p. 138.
12. *Ibid.*, p. 147.
13. I have used in this section many insights given by H. Mühlen, *op. cit.*

14. Dietrich von Hildebrand: *Metaphysik der Femeinschaft* (Regensberg: Habbel, 1955).
15. Wilhelm von Humboldt: *Gesammelte Schriften*; hrsg, v.d. Preuss Academic d. Wissenschafter (17 vols.; Berlin: B. Beher's Verlag, 1903-1936).
16. Wilhelm von Humboldt: *op. cit.*, art.: "Uber die Verwandschaft der Ortsadverbien mit dem Pronomen in einigen Sprache," p. 304 ff.

CHAPTER FOUR

1. Cf.: J.L. McKenzie: *Dictionary of the Bible* (N.Y.: Bruce Publishing Co., 1965): art.: "Spirit," pp. 840-842.
2. Yves Congar: *op. cit.*, Vol. 1, p. 3.
3. J. Danielou: "L'horizon patristique," cited by Congar, *op. cit.*, Vol. 1, p. 13, footnote 3.
4. Cf.: art.: "pneuma," in *Theological Dictionary of the New Testament*, G. Kittel & G. Friedrich (eds); by E. Schweizer, Vol. 6, (Grand Rapids: Eerdmans, 1964-1976), pp. 361-362; also *ibid.*, pp. 332-334, E. Schweizer's article on the Holy Spirit.
5. The author of the Yahwist tradition which begins at Gn 2:4 and ends with Nm 24:25 (naturally interspersed among other traditions, especially the Priestly) wrote sometime during the reign of Solomon (965-926 B.C.). This second creation account stresses man and his destiny as co-creator with God's Spirit, thus man's intimate and singular relationship with God's Spirit.
6. Emil Brunner: *Man in Revolt* (London, 1953), pp. 97-98.
7. Cf.: J. McKenzie: *op. cit.*, p. 694.
8. Eduard Schweizer: *The Holy Spirit*; tr. by Reginald H. and Ilse Fuller (Philadelphia: Fortress Press, 1980), pp. 24-25.
9. C. Larcher: *Etudes sur le Livre de la Sagesse* (Paris, 1969), p. 411, cited by Y. Congar *op. cit.*, Vol. 1, p. 10.
10. St. Gregory Nazianzus: *Oratio 31* in: *The Nicene & Post-Nicene Fathers* (NPNF), 2nd series; tr. by Philip Schaff and Henry Wace (Grand Rapids: Eerdmans, n.d.) Vol. 7, p. 327.

CHAPTER FIVE

1. St. Cyril of Alexandria, quoting St. Athanasius, said: "The Spirit is the perfect and natural image of the Son" in: *De Trinitate, PG,* Vol. 75; 1088B. Cf.: St. Athanasius: *Ad Serap.* I,20, in: *PG,* Vol. 26; 577B.
2. St. Irenaeus: *Adversus Haereses, op. cit.,* V, 28,4; p. 557, V, 6; pp. 531-532.
3. Cf.: Congar: *op. cit.,* Vol. 1, p. 15. Also George T. Montague, S.M.: *The Holy Spirit: Growth of a Biblical Tradition* (N.Y.: Paulist Press, 1976), p. 126.
4. Congar: *op. cit.,* p. 15.
5. Cf.: Alasdair I.C. Heron: *The Holy Spirit* (Philadelphia: Westminster Press, 1983), p. 39.
6. George Montague: *op. cit.,* p. 241.
7. On this theme cf.: J. Moltmann: *The Crucified God* (London: SCM Press, 1974), passim.
8. G. Montague: *op. cit.,* p. 308.
9. Cf.: J. McKenzie: *op. cit.,* p. 432.
10. Jerome Crowe, C.P.: *The Acts,* in: *New Testament Message,* Vol. 8 (Wilmington: Glazier, Inc., 1979), p. 15.
11. *Ibid.,* p. 14.
12. Cf.: A. Heron: *op. cit.,* p. 53.
13. Augustine: *In Evangelium Joannis Tractatus,* 120, 3, in: *CCL (Corpus Christianorum, Series Latina)* (Paris, 1953 ff.), Vol. 36, p. 661.
14. G. Montague: *op. cit.,* p. 355.
15. Cf.: F. Porsch: *Pneuma und Wort* (Frankfurt, 1974), pp. 237 ff. Also cf.: I. de la Potterie: *La vie selon l'Esprit. Condition du Chrétien,* in the series: *Unam Sanctam,* no. 55 (Paris, 1965).
16. *op. cit.,* Vol. 1, pp. 54-56.
17. Cf.: C. Moule: *op. cit.,* pp. 40-42; A. Heron: *op. cit.,* pp. 45-46; G. Maloney: *The Cosmic Christ from Paul to Teilhard* (N.Y.: Sheed and Ward, 1968), pp. 21ff; G. Montague: *op. cit.,* pp. 206 ff.

18. For Paul's concept of resurrectional life even now and in the life to come, cf.: G. Maloney: *The First Day of Eternity: Resurrection Now* (N.Y.: Crossroad, 1982), pp. 78 ff.

CHAPTER SIX

1. Louis John Cameli: "Spirit," in *Chicago Studies* (Spring, 1976), Vol. 15, no. 1, p. 85.
2. St. Athanasius: *Contra Gentes*, 41, p. 26, in *Post-Nicene Fathers of the Christian Church* (Grand Rapids, MI: Eerdmans, 1957).
3. St. Athanasius: *Ad Seraph*, I, 20, in *PG*, Vol. 26; 577B. See also: St. Cyril of Alexandria: *De Trinitate* in *PG*, Vol. 75; 1088B.
4. Teilhard de Chardin: *The Phenomenon of Man*, tr. Bernard Wall (London: Wm. Collins Sons & Co., 1959), pp. 264-267.

CHAPTER SEVEN

1. Bede Jarrett, O.P.: *The Abiding Presence of the Holy Ghost in the Soul* (Westminster, MD: The Newman Press, 1957), p. 34.
2. Cf.: Yves Congar, O.P.: *The Mystery of the Temple* (London, 1962). pp. 11, 12, 17 ff., 132, 297-298, note 5.
3. Y. Congar: *I Believe. op. cit.*, Vol. 2, p. 80.
4. Luis M. Bermejo, S.J.: *op. cit.*, p. 75.
5. *Ibid.*, p. 81.
6. Jean Galot: *L'Esprit d'Amour* (Brussels: Desclée de Brouwer, 1958); tr. my own, p. 147.
7. Thomas Aquinas: *De Veritate*: 27,2 and 7.
8. Thomas: *Summa Theologica*: 1-11, Q.110, a.4.
9. *Ibid.*, 1-11, Q.109, intro., a.2; Q.110, a.1.
10. Karl Rahner: *The Trinity*, tr. Joseph Donceel (N.Y.: Herder & Herder, 1970), p. 23.
11. Rahner: *Nature and Grace*, tr. Dinah Wharton (London: Sheed & Ward, 1963), p. 24.

12. Rahner: *The Trinity*, p. 101.
13. Cf.: Luis Bermejo: *op. cit.*, p. 169 ff.
14. Vladimir Lossky: *The Mystical Theology of the Eastern Church* (London: James Clarke & Co., 1957), p. 172.
15. Peter Fransen, S.J.: *Divine Grace and Man* (N.Y.: Desclée Co., 1962), p. 72.
16. Bermejo: *op. cit.*, p. 169.
17. St. Augustine: *Confessions*; Bk. 10,32; tr. by Mary T. Clark, in the Series: *The Classics of Western Spirituality* (N.Y.: Paulist Press, 1984), p. 149: *Selected Writings of St. Augustine*.

CHAPTER EIGHT

1. *Byzantine Daily Worship*, ed. by Archbishop Joseph Raya and Dr. Jose De Vinck (Allendale, NJ: Alleluia Press, 1968), pp. 898-899.
2. Cf.: J. Mahe: "La Sanctification d'apres saint Cyrille d'Alexandrie," in: *Revue d'histoire ecclesiastique* (Paris, 1909, Vol. 10, p. 480).
3. St. Cyril of Alexandria: *Thesaurus*, 24, p. 75:597 C.
4. Concerning holiness, cf. my work *God's Incredible Mercy* (Staten Island, N.Y.: Alba House, 1989), Chapter Two: "Holy, Holy, Holy, Lord God!" pp. 27-52.
5. St. Athanasius: *De Incarnatione*, 2, 54; pp. 25, 192; St. Irenaeus: *Adversus Haereses*, III, 19, 1, in *The Ante-Nicene Fathers*, I, *op. cit.*, pp. 448-449.
6. For writers who have developed this theme consult: G.A. Maloney, S.J.: *Man — The Divine Icon* (Pecos, MN: Dove Press, 1973); Sr. Maria Ryk: "The Holy Spirit's Role in the Deification of Man According to Contemporary Orthodox Theology (1925-1972)" in: *Diakonia*, Vol. 10, nos. 1 & 2, 1975, 24-39; 109-130; Myrrha Lot-Borodine: *La deification de l'homme selon la doctrine des Péres grecs* (Paris: Cerf, 1970); L. Janssens: "Notre filiation divine d'apres saint Cyrille d'Alexandrie," in: *Ephemerides theologicae Lovanienses*, Vol. 15 (1938); pp. 233-278.

7. The most complete synthesis on this topic has been worked out by Thomas Aquinas: in III Sent. d. 34 7 35; *Summa Theologiae*; Ia; IIae, q. 58-70 and in ST IIa IIae. For the history of the development of the gifts of the Spirit cf.: G. Bardy and F. Vandenbroucke in *Dictionnaire de spiritualité*, Vol. III: "Les dons de Saint-Esprit" (Paris, 1954), cols. 1579-1603.

8. *Op. cit.*, Vol. 2, p. 134.

9. For a popular and even devotional treatment of the gifts, fruits and virtues cf.: Luis M. Martinez, *The Sanctifier* (Patterson, NJ: St. Anthony's Guild, 1957), tr. by Sr. M. Aquinas, OSU.

10. Thomas Aquinas: *ST IIa IIae*, q. 8.

11. *ST Ia IIae*, q. 70.

12. L. Cerfaux: *The Christian in the Theology of St. Paul* (London, 1967), pp. 461 ff.

13. There are other lists of the fruit of the Spirit. Cf.: Eph 5:9; 1 Tm 6:11; Rm 17; 2 Cor 6:6-7 given by Paul. Cf. also: Jm 3:17-18.

14. Cf. Congar: *op. cit.*, Vol. 2, p. 138.

15. Alfred Delp, S.J.: *Facing Death* (London, 1962), pp. 178-179, cited by Congar: *op. cit.*, p. 127.

CHAPTER NINE

1. This and other related themes have been developed in my book: *Mysticism and the New Age: A Christic Consciousness toward a New Creation* (Staten Island, N.Y.: Alba House, 1990).

2. P.C. Mozoomdar: *The Spirit of God* (Boston: George Ellis, 1894), pp. 18-19.

3. Petro B.T. Bilaniuk: *Theology and Economy of the Holy Spirit* (Bangalore, India: Dharmaram Publications, 1980), p. 83.

4. Bishop Cassian: "The Family of God," in: *The Ecumenical Review*, Vol. 9 (1957), pp. 129-142.

5. F.X. Durrwell, C.SS.R.: *The Resurrection*, tr. by Rosemary Sheed (N.Y.: Sheed & Ward, 1966), p. 210.

6. Further development of these themes can be found in: Joseph Bonsiren, S.J. *Theology of the New Testament* (Westminster, MD: Newman Press, 1962); Pierre Benoit: "Corps, tête, et

plerome dans les Epitres de la Captivité," in: *Les Epitres de la Captivité* (Paris: Beauchesne, 1935), pp. 40 ff.

7. P. Benoit: art. cit., p. 147.

8. Yves Congar: *Jesus Christ*, tr. by Luke O'Neill (N.Y.: Herder & Herder, 1966), pp. 193-194.

9. Cf.: the excellent teaching on the four signs of the Church of Christ as one, holy, catholic and apostolic of Yves Congar: *op. cit.: I Believe*, Vol. 2, pp. 15-64.

10. Cf.: G.A. Maloney: "Epiklesis" in: *The New Catholic Encyclopedia*, Vol. 5, pp. 464-466.

11. St. Basil: *De Spiritu Sancto*: PG 32; 133 C.

12. Cf.: *Lumen Gentium*, 48, 1,9; *Gaudium et Spes*, 45; *Ad Gentes*, 1 & 5.

13. E. Schillebeeckx, O.P.: *The Church and Mankind*, in: *Concilium*, Vol. 1 (N.Y.: Paulist Press, 1965), pp. 84-85.

14. *Lumen Gentium*, 10.

15. This example is inspired by E. Schillebeeckx: *Christ the Sacrament of the Encounter with God* (N.Y.: Sheed & Ward, 1963), pp. 215-216.

16. Karl Rahner: *Mission et Grace*, I, "XXe siecle, siecle de grace," in: *Collection Siecle et catholicisme* (Brussels, Mame, 1962), p. 213.

17. See my chapter 7: "The Role of Christianity in Building a Better World," in my work: *Mysticism and the New Age: A Christic Consciousness toward a New Creation* (Staten Island, N.Y.: Alba House, 1990). Also: Walbert Buhlmann: *The Coming of the Third Church*, tr. by Ralph Woodhall and A.N. (Maryknoll, N.Y.: Orbis Books, 1976); Vincent Cosmao: *Changing the World: An Agenda for the Churches* (Maryknoll: Orbis Books, 1984).

18. Cf.: Vatican II's decree: *On Ecumenism*, no. 6.

19. *Lumen Gentium*, no. 12.

20. Heribert Mühlen: "The Charismatic Renewal as Experience," in: *The Holy Spirit and Power: The Catholic Charismatic Renewal*, ed. by Killian McDonnell, OSB (N.Y.: Doubleday, 1975), p. 108.

21. In regard to the use of Pentecostal and charismatic cf.: Y. Congar, *op. cit.*, Vol. 2, pp. 161 ff.; Francis Sullivan, S.J.: "The Ecclesiological Context of Charismatic Renewal," in: *The Holy Spirit and Power, op. cit.*, pp. 119-138. Some suggested bibliography dealing in general with this renewal: K. Ranaghan: *Catholic Pentecostals* (New Jersey, 1969); E. O'Connor: *The Pentecostal Movement in the Catholic Church* (Notre Dame, IN: 1971); *Theological and Pastoral Orientations on the Catholic Charismatic Renewal* (Malines Document: Notre Dame, 1974); Leon Joseph Cardinal Suenens: *A New Pentecost* tr. by Francis Martin (N.Y.: Seabury, 1974); René Laurentin: *Catholic Pentecostalism* (London, 1977); Yves Congar: *I Believe in the Holy Spirit*, 3 vols., (N.Y., 1983); Peter Hocken: *New Heaven, New Earth? An Encounter with Pentecostalism* (London, 1976); W. Hollenwager: *The Pentecostals: the Charismatic Movement in the Churches* (Philadelphia, 2nd ed., 1973).

22. On discernment cf.: Jules Toner, S.J.: *A Commentary on St. Ignatius' Rules for the Discernment of Spirits: A Guide to the Principles and Practice* (St. Louis: The Institute of Jesuit Sources, 1982); Richard Hauser: *In His Spirit: A Guide to Today's Spirituality* (N.Y.: Paulist Press, 1982); *Moving in the Spirit* (N.Y.: Paulist Press, 1986); Karl Rahner: *The Dynamic Element in the Church* (N.Y.: Herder & Herder, 1964); John Futrell, S.J.: "Communal Discernment: Reflections on Experience," in: *Studies in the Spirituality of Jesuits*; Vol. 4, no. 5, Nov. 1972, pp. 159-194.

23. A fine example of a modern examen of conscience, cf.: George Aschenbrenner, S.J.: "Consciousness Examen," in: *Review for Religious*, Vol. 31, no. 1 (1972), pp. 14-21.

24. St. John of the Cross's advice is the standard for discerning sense experiences in prayer: *The Ascent of Mount Carmel*, Book II; Ch. 11, pp. 131 ff. in: *The Collected Works of St. John of the Cross*, tr. by Kieran Kavanaugh and Otilio Rodriguez (Washington, D.C.: ICS Publications, 1973.)

25. St. Symeon the New Theologian: *Hymns of Divine Love*, tr. by G.A. Maloney, S.J. (Denville, NJ: Dimension Books, 1975), Hymn 44, pp. 231-232.